There is no good ... ...Daniel from
... was taken
... ...e
... ...om a visit

Daniel, looking unusually clean
and well-brushed, and his friends Alastair
and Jamie Boddington, at the birthday
party of their younger brother,
Nicky. *Adrian Boddington*

Swinging forward into life. Daniel on
holiday in Wales, soon after the Diary ends.

Helen Farquhar-
Thomson.
1992.

THE DANIEL
DIARY

THE DANIEL DIARY

Ailsa Fabian

Foreword by Dora Black

GRAFTON BOOKS

A Division of the Collins Publishing Group

LONDON GLASGOW
TORONTO SYDNEY AUCKLAND

Grafton Books
A Division of the Collins Publishing Group
8 Grafton Street, London W 1 X 3LA

Published by Grafton Books 1988

Copyright © Ailsa Fabian 1988

British Library Cataloguing in Publication Data
Fabian, Ailsa
The Daniel diary.
1. Bereavement in children
I. Title
306.8'8   BF723.G75

ISBN 0-246-13307-4

Photoset in Great Britain by
Rowland Phototypesetting Limited, Bury St Edmunds, Suffolk
and printed by
Robert Hartnoll (1985) Limited,
Bodmin, Cornwall

All rights reserved. No part of this publication may be
reproduced, stored in a retrieval system, or transmitted,
in any form or by any means, electronic, mechanical,
photocopying, recording or otherwise, without the prior
permission of the publisher.

The verse from 'The Song of the Mad Prince' by
Walter de la Mare is reproduced by permission of
the Literary Trustees of Walter de la Mare and
the Society of Authors as their representative.

To Daniel

FOREWORD

I read this book with rapt absorption and great pleasure. It is beautifully written and, even more important, a genuine and sensitive contemporaneous observation of a young child's attempts to grapple with the sudden death of his beloved older sister – helped by a mother who respected him and was herself trying to find a way of coming to terms with her own loss.

The beautifully described and painfully honest account of her struggle to explain the unexplainable – her exploration through discussions with friends and through reading the professional literature, will be of immense help to those who find themselves in her shoes and counsellors and others concerned with helping bereaved children. She finds herself trapped into maintaining a story to which she is no longer able to commit herself – that the angels took Sarah's spirit to heaven – as Daniel's growing ability to reason makes it untenable for her. But above all this vivid diary gives us a unique insight into the immensely long and active odyssey of a young child – not yet three – to come to terms with his sister's death. I can do no better than quote the author's Introduction, 'Each time I re-read the Diary, it seems to me almost unbearably charged with sorrow and I wonder why any outsider should want to share so much pain. The reward for those who do is to share also the courage, intelligence, and poetic imagination with which a young child was able to confront tragedy.'

Dora Black, MB, FRCPsych, DPM
Consultant Child Psychiatrist, Royal Free Hospital
Vice-chairman of Cruse, the Organisation for the Bereaved

Who said, 'Peacock Pie'?
   The old King to the sparrow:
Who said, 'Crops are ripe'?
   Rust to the harrow:
Who said, 'Where sleeps she now?
   Where rests she now her head,
Bathed in eve's loveliness'? –
   That's what I said.

Walter de la Mare

INTRODUCTION

When our daughter Sarah died suddenly at the age of five, Erwin and I shared the desolation in equal measure. Knowing that there was not a hair's breadth between us, we were able to acknowledge our common grief over and over again, without words, or in the tritest of phrases. This was my deepest source of strength in learning to endure a loss for which there is no consolation. We also had to continue looking after our second child Daniel, then not quite three, and running a household which included my father and my mother-in-law. It was due to this sharing and these responsibilities that I didn't break down and take to my bed.

But at such a time one needs every support one can get. In the struggle to keep going with at least the appearance of normality, I clung to the routines of daily life, and to three of them in particular – housework, drink, and writing. Housework was humble and undemanding. I hoovered the sitting-room floor with a dim and faintly comforting sense that I was helping to maintain the fabric of living. Drink divided the bleak future into manageable segments, and a couple of whiskies every evening before dinner became something to look forward to as the afternoon dragged on; if I then went to bed early with a sleeping tablet, the respite lasted until four o'clock next morning, when the knowledge that she was dead pierced through my sleep like a search-light. Writing enabled me to live a double life, detaching myself from experience while remaining immersed in it.

After a month or so, housework lost its power to soothe and became once more just a chore. By the end of a year I had given up sleeping tablets and the desperate resort to drink. Writing has remained an enduring resource. Writing, I mean, not just in the public sense of elaborating texts for others to read, but as the basic activity of covering paper with words. I began to compile a record of Sarah's life, setting down in detail everything that I could remember about her. I took up again a practice that had helped in moments of crisis ever since school days, of keeping a journal of self-observation. Soon it multiplied into a number of separate journals written in different modes. I copied extracts from books and wrote voluminous commentaries on them. And I started making the notes that eventually turned into this Diary, which record Daniel's comments and questions about his sister's death during the months and years which followed.

It began almost by chance. On the second evening after she died, when Daniel had been put to bed, I sat down to get on with my self-appointed task of fixing on paper everything I remembered about Sarah, and found myself instead writing about Daniel. We had taken him that afternoon to the hospital to see her body, and while we were sitting forlornly round the table after our return, he evoked her vanished presence in words that I found very moving. They form the first entry in the Diary. I scribbled an account of the afternoon's events, and having thus begun, I continued during the following months to write down whatever Daniel said about Sarah, the conversations we had together, and the games and gestures which seemed to speak of her or of death. Soon there were enough notes to put into a separate file, which I labelled 'Daniel and Sarah'.

I accumulated the notes without any thought of publication, but the impulse behind them was the same as that which compelled me to write Sarah's life-story. For me, her life had been a constantly unfolding revelation of the essential humanity possessed by a child from the first day of infancy. I wanted to share that revelation, but the scenes which had bestowed it were losing their sharpness, and many had already vanished from memory. At times I felt that I had forgotten everything except my own sense of wonder. By recording Daniel's exact words, I could preserve evidence of the same spontaneous human virtues that had astonished me in her.

We were living at the time in Melbourne, in the rambling, ungainly house in which I had grown up, there on a visit from London which had lengthened into a stay of several years because of a wrangle over a family business. During the remainder of our time in Melbourne, Daniel talked often about Sarah and I continued to make notes. When finally we returned to London more than two years later, I brought my files with me, and, once settled back in the flat where Daniel had been born and Sarah had spent half her life, I went on writing. But now there was seldom anything to add to the Daniel and Sarah file; Daniel was going to school, absorbed in experiences he had never shared with her, and gradually forgetting their years together. Eventually, needing more space in the filing cabinet, I put the notes into a large brown envelope, stowed it away on top of the wardrobe with a pile of similar packages, and forgot about it.

Years later, when Daniel had left school and was wandering the world, I rediscovered them while rummaging among the dusty envelopes for something else. I read some of the entries with surprise and pleasure, beginning to wonder whether I couldn't do something with them. I assumed at first that what I had was raw material, fascinating but shapeless, needing to be sifted, worked on, and supplemented. It was only when I had transcribed the untidy pile of pages, giving them the unity of a neat typescript, that I saw that what I had was already a self-sustaining structure and an almost complete story. I began to refer to it as the Daniel Diary. I thought of it as a 'found object', comparable to the piece of weathered wood or twisted iron which a sculptor transforms into a work of art by isolating and presenting it as such. I had written the individual notes but not the Diary, choosing the incidents to record but never reading through the growing accumulation to study its shape. The fact that I wasn't writing *a* diary, but at least three concurrently, sorting out from the spate of words as I went along what belonged to each, gave it unity. Life itself, through Daniel's growing understanding and mastery of the tragedy that had befallen him, gave it shape. It appeared to need only the addition of a brief factual introduction.

At first I assumed that this would have to include a description of the relationship between Sarah and Daniel during her lifetime. Who could understand the depth of his grief without knowing of the love and happiness they had shared? I looked through the notes I had made after Sarah's death, but I found that I had written about Daniel there only as her little brother, seeing him through her eyes. Now I wanted to alter the perspective and show Sarah as she had been for Daniel, but the scenes that might have shown this had vanished with the passage of time and the work of shaping memory for a different purpose. When I read the Diary again, I saw that it didn't matter. Daniel's own words of longing for Sarah, and his evocations of their days together, are sufficient evidence of their mutual happiness. But one of my notes about Sarah provides a background to the Diary's first entry. It describes a favourite game which Daniel was to recall often.

14

On ordinary days, when we were at home, the children's dinner-time boisterousness evolved into the marvellous after-dinner game of Chasey. We had only to appear in one of the four doorways that linked the downstairs rooms in a circle, and call out, 'Chasey!' to start them off. 'Look out, Daniel,' Sarah called. 'They're coming! Run for your life!' She was the more agile, darting and changing direction like a hare, while Daniel trotted solidly after her. When we pulled the obvious trick of appearing suddenly in front of them, instead of behind, Sarah turned so swiftly that she cannoned into Daniel and they collapsed softly like a pair of puppies. The beauty of the game was that we need hardly do more than step from one foot to the other for them to race off again, encouraging each other with shrill screams, at once gleeful and apprehensive.

Sarah loved Erwin to catch her, and she would run full tilt into his arms, go limp so that he couldn't hold her, then wriggle free and be off again. Or, instead, she would call, 'He's an old camel. Get up beast! Gee-up! Hey-up!' in a broad rustic accent copied from Erwin. The beast, swaying and rocking under his double load and belaboured with fists and heels, pounded round the room on all fours, while I had a welcome rest and we all shrieked with laughter.

Sarah's disappearance from this scene was devastatingly sudden. One evening she seemed rather grizzly and had a slight temperature, so I put her to bed in my room. She remained there throughout the next day, with a mounting fever and distressing spells of laboured breathing, but between these she seemed her usual lively self, joking with Daniel when he visited her, and offering him a share of the jelly beans and ice-cream which the doctor had prescribed. In the evening we were advised to take her to hospital. Daniel came with me as I carried her down the drive to the ambulance, and stood with Erwin waving goodbye with outward cheerfulness as we drove off. Neither Erwin nor I had acknowledged to ourselves the terror we felt, and I don't think we can have conveyed it to Daniel. She died that same night. I must have told Daniel next day that she had died and would never come back to us, but I don't recall when or how. Most of the events of that day have mercifully vanished from memory. On the second day, the Diary takes up the story.

It records a time of grief, that state in which one simultaneously believes and disbelieves in a death. In this respect Daniel and I were identical. A child's grief no doubt differs from that of an adult in many ways (notably in sheer density of knowledge), but in essence they are the same. When Daniel on that first night sadly recalled the lost games of chasey, I am convinced that he knew already he would never see her again, and that the knowledge never thereafter left him for long. His optimistic visions that she had returned, or that she would soon return, were more vivid and convincing than my similar imaginings, but not much more enduring.

Each time I reread the Diary, it seems to me almost unbearably charged with sorrow, and I wonder why any outsider should want to share so much pain. The reward for those who do is to share also the courage, intelligence, and poetic imagination with which a young child was able to confront tragedy.

1964

June 16

Dinner tonight, the first meal we have eaten together without her. Her chair was there, empty. Daniel sat beside me. He has looked very quiet and subdued since I talked to him this morning about going to see Sarah. He said, sadly and quietly, sitting at the table, 'I heard someone say "Chasey!"'

In the afternoon, Erwin and I had taken Mama and Daniel to the hospital to see Sarah's body. I had told Daniel that we were going to see her, but that it wouldn't really be Sarah any more, that she wouldn't be able to move or to speak or to recognise us.

A nurse took us to a room near the chapel. Sarah lay on a bed, behind a curtain which the nurse drew back. Her eyes were closed, her forehead pale, and her cheeks bluish, but her hair and the curve of her cheek were unchanged. One of her bears was tucked under the sheet beside her, and on the pillow lay the hospital's tribute of a plastic rosebud. I touched her forehead and then lifted Daniel to see her.

'That's Sarah.'

Daniel, in a deep voice with a musical lift and fall at the end: 'Yes, it i-is.'

I placed beside her the little reading-book *Monkey*, which we would soon have started together, when we had finished the one before, *Horse*. I had brought it from home. I didn't want to stay longer; it wasn't Sarah; but Mama

17

and Erwin, in continuance of a family tradition, wanted to sketch her, so I took Daniel by the hand and we wandered off into the hospital lobby, where there was a children's playroom.

As we were leaving the room, Erwin picked up Sarah's bear from the bed.

Daniel objected, 'Hey, don't take Sarah's bear away!'

So Erwin let it remain until later, when Daniel was not there to see.

June 18

Daniel very tired yesterday evening. We had been out all afternoon and by the time we got home he was listless and pale and unnoticing, then got angry when his new crane wouldn't do what he wanted it to. He stayed up while we had dinner, not hungry but irritable and unreasonable. I took him up to bed and asked him what story he wanted.

'I don't know.'

When I offered to read *Little Engine* he got very cross.

'I don't want it.'

He didn't want the light off, or to go to bed.

'What do you want?'

Daniel, in a very flat, deep, hoarse voice, 'I don't want anything.'

But I did read him several stories and we played little games. I tucked him up several times, but he didn't fall asleep. Once I came downstairs, because Erwin wasn't well, but Daniel came down too, and wanted to play in the playroom. I took him upstairs again and read another story, but he was tense and didn't want to sleep. I rocked him on my knee and sang 'Pat-a-cake, pat-a-cake, baker's man, Bake me a cake as fast as you can! Prick it and pat it and mark it with D, And put it in the oven for Daniel and me.' He smiled and was soothed and calmed. I sang it four or five times. Then I changed it to 'Put it in the oven for Sarah and me.' He looked suddenly happy, and I had to repeat it twenty times. Whenever I sang 'Daniel and me', or even if he thought I was going to, he said 'Sing Sarah!' and smiled.

June 19, 9 a.m.
Daniel, playing with his crane on the floor, 'Look at Sarah and Daniel! And Mummy and Daddy! Look at the crane! Look at Sarah and Daniel!'

'What are Sarah and Daniel doing?'

Daniel didn't reply, but smiled happily and rather coyly. A little later I overheard: '"Who's making that noise?" said Sarah. "The crane is making that noise. It went right up." "Oh!" said Sarah.'

In the afternoon, to me: 'Is Sarah better yet?'

To Betty [*my sister, who lived nearby and whom we saw often*]: 'I always make Sarah laugh.'

June 20
'Do you want a banana?'
   'No.'
   'Do you want a piece of cheese?'
   'No.'
   'Do you want a hot milk drink?'
   'No.'
   'What do you want?'
   'I don't want anything.'

At bedtime the same day, 'Are you Mummy's little boy?'
   'No.'

The same question and reply for Grandma, Grandpa, Sarah, Aunty Betty.

'Who are you?'

'I'm not anybody. I'm just an animal with a big beak.'

June 21

'Are you Mummy's boy?'

'No. I'm Sarah's boy.'

Betty, referring to the expected arrival of Erwin's sister Ruth who was flying from New York to be with us: 'Do you know who's coming tomorrow?'

'Yes, Sarah.'

Later, he asked me, 'Why don't we go to the hospital and bring Sarah home?'

June 23

Yesterday, the day of the funeral, was a strange and bewildering day for Daniel. He woke up alone in his bedroom for the seventh day since Sarah died. We were already up and dressed and he came downstairs by himself. If he looked into our room on the way, he would have seen the beds already neatly made, the first time such a thing has ever happened so early. Erwin and I were ready to leave for the hospital. [*Sarah's body had remained there since she died, and the funeral was to start from there.*] I took him to Grandpa, who was having breakfast, and he stayed quietly with him, sitting on his knee. But he looked out the window as we passed and saw us drive away.

Molly, the nurse, should have arrived at 8.30 to look after him but she did not turn up. I don't blame her. She has only been with us two weeks. It was a bit much to ask a young girl who barely knew us to experience the sudden

death of her charge, and then to go on ministering to a
fraught household and a bereaved child. When Betty
came to collect Grandpa for the funeral and found no
nurse, she rang Jenny Boddington across the street, and
hastily got Daniel dressed. Betty said to him, 'Jenny is
coming to take you over to play with Alastair and Nicho-
las,' and he didn't protest, although he had never been
there alone before, only once with me when I called in for a
cup of coffee with Jenny after taking the children to school.

We returned from the funeral soon after 11. Maggie and
Ed asked where he was and suggested we go and get him.
When I rang the doorbell I could hear a child crying
inside, but it wasn't Daniel, it was Alastair. Daniel looked
stricken and subdued, as Sarah had looked when I called
for her at lunchtime during her brief attendance at Man-
ningtree Road State School. He held out his arms to me
and I carried him back, while Ed and Maggie carried the
cranes and tractors. In the sitting room there were
perhaps a dozen people standing drinking coffee.

He said in a rather puzzled way, 'There's a party!'

He knew everyone, but pointed to Douglas, whom he
knew least, and said, 'Who is that?'

He didn't rest after lunch but stayed with us, talking to
Ruth [*Erwin's sister*], who had arrived as the funeral guests
were leaving, and playing with the crane, quiet but with
little outbursts of crossness. At dinner-time he wouldn't
eat and was restless. He climbed on my knee and in a
sudden spurt of rage scratched my neck with his finger-
nails so that it hurt.

Later, when I was changing his clothes for bed, I said,
'You're a cross boy, aren't you?'

'Yes,' he said, 'I scratched you!'

At bedtime Erwin helped him upstairs and tried to
clean his teeth and read a story, although he didn't know
what story he wanted. When it was my turn and I asked

him what story I should read he said, 'I don't know. I don't want anything. I don't know what story I want.' I read to him from *Sara and Hoppity*, a pedestrian collection of stories that both he and Sarah had often asked for. I tried to put him to bed after a long story, gave in to his demand for another, and then tried again. He cried, yelled for more stories, and threw his bears violently on to the floor one after another.

Suddenly, without any planning, I started to talk to him.

I said, 'You're missing Sarah, aren't you, Daniel?'

'Yes.'

'We are too. We miss her very much indeed, our beautiful Sarah. Daddy does and Mummy does and so do Grandma and Grandpa. But Sarah was so very very sick that she couldn't come home. She isn't in the hospital any more. She had to go away because she was so very sick.'

'Where is Sarah?'

'She's up with the angels. She's a very long way away.'

'What's it like with the angels?'

'No one knows very much. Only people who are very very sick and old people go there.'

'Couldn't the doctor go there in his car and get her?'

He listened quietly and asked serious questions. We talked for a long time. I told him that we had all been that morning to say goodbye to Sarah, and talked about her. He lay on her bed, and I said, 'Sarah used to say "Make sure I'm nicely tucked up before you clean your teeth, and after. See you later alligator."'

Daniel, in a deep voice, 'Yes, she did.'

I tucked him into his own cot and sat beside him, still talking about Sarah.

Suddenly he asked 'Hey, what was it she went away to hospital in? I can't say it.'

'The ambulance?'

'Yes.'

Once he screamed out desperately three times, 'I want Sarah,' but most of the time he listened attentively, or asked solemn questions. After a while he said, 'Sing Rock-a-bye Baby.' I rocked him on my knee and sang it three or four times. Then he said, 'Sing the other one, sing Baker's Man.' I sang several times, 'Put it in the oven for Sarah and me.' He listened closely, and when once I sang 'for Daniel', he said impatiently, 'No! Sing Sarah!' Then I put him back in the cot and he lay on his side and immediately fell asleep. I had been talking to him for almost an hour.

These songs were re-introduced only a few nights ago, when I suddenly thought that we were demanding too much of him, and that after such a shock he should have the comfort of babying of a kind he hadn't had since he was less than a year old. I used to sing 'Rock-a-bye Baby' to him then. [*But I notice only now, as I type out these lines, what a curiously ambiguous song it is, with such menace underlying its soothing rhythm – 'When the bough breaks the cradle will fall. Down will come baby, cradle and all.'*] I put Sarah's name into 'Pat-a-cake' because I knew he must be thinking of her, and felt that it would help him if her name were openly spoken.

Next morning Daniel came into our bedroom a little later than usual, looking calm and almost happy. Erwin brought us up some breakfast, and he drank a full mug of milk. Then we walked downstairs hand in hand. On the way he asked, 'Where's Sarah gone?' with no eagerness in his voice, but in a calm and accepting way, as if asking for confirmation of last night's conversation.

I said, 'She's gone with the angels, a long way away.'

He waited a moment and then said, 'Sarah wore a dress.'

'Yes, she liked to wear dresses and she looked very pretty in them, didn't she?'

'Yes, she did.'

Later in the day he asked me, about the angels, 'Do they live up in the mountains?'

June 24

Daniel sometimes talks freely and easily about Sarah. Last night, when he was playing with Mama, I heard him say, 'If Sarah was here, she would say hullo to all the birds.' They were looking at a book of photographs. This morning as we came down the stairs, 'Sarah used to like to hold your hand, coming down the stairs.'

At lunch-time I cut up an orange into sections to give him. He named the sections 'orange bunnies', by analogy with the small squares of bread and honey which recently have been called 'honey bunnies'.

Daniel, 'Once when Beverly was here, Sarah said she would like some mandarin bunnies, and Beverly got a mandarin and made her some mandarin bunnies.'

I took Daniel out to say goodnight to the gardener before his rest. The gardener, a shy young man, asked where Sarah was.

'Sarah's not with us any more. She died. About a week ago,' I replied.

He looked astounded and embarrassed. 'Of natural causes?'

'Yes. She died of flu.'

Daniel watched my face and looked very grave. We have by now talked quite a lot about it, but speaking to a comparative stranger must have given some further reality to the fantastic and terrible story of Sarah's death.

24

I said, 'You look sad, Daniel, and it is sad. We are all very sad.'

Sarah was so much in the forefront of our attention that in some ways she overshadowed Dan. It was her growing understanding of the world that we fostered and watched over, her love and eagerness that we wanted to protect. I realised this with a shock tonight when Dan asked, listening to a conversation between me and Ruth, 'What's a mammal?' I haven't been used to receiving such questions from him. He had to tag along behind Sarah and pick up what he could from listening to our talk with her. I don't know whether this made him better or worse off. It was a very secure existence.

June 25
Daniel in the bathroom preparing to go to bed, 'Hey, let's go and bring Sarah home from the angels.'
  His face lit up with new hope. Yet we have had to tell him over and over again during the past few days that it is impossible for us to bring her home. The last time was this morning, in the car as we were returning home after collecting Sarah's ashes – although he didn't know that that was our errand.

June 26
Someone suggested that we ask Beverly to visit us. [*Beverly had been the children's nurse, and a great favourite. She had left us about six weeks before, to be married.*]
  Daniel: 'Yes, we'll get Sarah home from the angels when she's better again, and Beverly will come to see us.'

June 27, Saturday morning

Daniel cross and doesn't know what he wants. As we waited in the supermarket car-park for Erwin, he wanted me to show him the aerial on another car. When I did, he cried and said he wanted to see a different aerial. I took him back to the car, saying I had already shown him the aerial.

'No you didn't.'

We were to return home in two cars because we had picked up Grandpa's Daimler from the garage. Daniel didn't know which he wanted to go in, really wanting us all to stay together. In the end he came with me, Erwin following in the Daimler.

I said, 'Look, Daddy's just behind.'

'No he isn't.'

A mood in which he refused to acknowledge anything right with the world.

When we got home I gave him an aeroplane-swing on the lawn, he went briefly out in the car with Grandpa, watched the fish cooking for lunch, and ate a good lunch of fish and milk, but telling us not to look at him. After lunch he asked for his big red elephant. I went and got it, saying as I gave it to him, 'That elephant was a present from Sarah, wasn't it?'

'Yes, it was,' he agreed.

When I took him upstairs for his rest, he got furious because he wanted all the blinds raised right to the top of the windows, but one wouldn't go right up. I said to him, 'You're not really cross. You're sad because Sarah's not here.' I had just read a letter from Cecily [*my close friend Cecily de Monchaux, Reader in Psychology at University College London, and a practising psychoanalyst*] in which she suggested that his sorrow for Sarah might take the form of anger, something I had seen for myself during the morning.

'You want your Sarah and she can't be here,' I continued.

'No I don't. I don't want Sarah.'

'Well it has its good side too. You used to be the little boy and now you're the big boy.'

'Yes, I'm the big boy now.'

June 28

After a long stretch when he never knew what he wanted, for the past three or four nights Daniel has asked both Erwin and me to read him a story called *The Happy Little Whale*. Erwin pointed out that it is a fable of loss and reunion – about a little whale separated from her companions at sea and taken off to an aquarium, where she is very lonely until given a new playmate just her size. Tonight I read the last line wrongly – 'They squeak for joy, those happy little whales.'

Daniel corrected me. 'No, those *two* happy little whales.'

It is a rather horrid little story, flatly written, whitewashing the plight of animals in captivity. Ruth overheard it one night and was appalled at its triteness.

'Can't you get him some of the classic children's stories?' she asked.

But literary quality isn't the supreme value just now, and the ridiculous Happy Little Whale is precisely what he needs.

Daniel's love-offerings of urine. He has wee'd beside a farm tractor when we were buying apples on the road to Portsea, alongside an enormous road-working machine parked some distance from our car on the Portland trip, on the railway lines in the sawmill during the last Sunday outing beyond Marysville. Last week he wouldn't wee in the lavatory when I was getting him ready for bed – then ran into the bedroom and cheerfully wee'd on the floor beside Sarah's bed.

June 29

I started these notes to record everything that can be remembered of Sarah, but I spend a lot of time writing down observations of Dan. It is obvious and inevitable – new life unfolds and the dead are left behind. But it is very painful and I don't want it to happen.

Daniel has made several leaps forward towards maturity in the two weeks since Sarah died:
– Attempts to understand what it means when I tell him she died.
– Getting himself out of bed in the morning (not entirely unprecedented), and carrying his basket of tractors into my room, and even once downstairs (quite new).
– Pooing in the lavatory, which he had never done before, with pride in the achievement.
– Talking more, and saying more complex things.

He has always had a concern to pronounce words correctly. This morning at breakfast he said to me, 'What is it, Bressleton? I can't say it.' He had to repeat it several times before I understood. I said 'Bretherton', slowly. He repeated it after me, pronouncing the *th* quite correctly. A few days ago he had said the same thing about the word 'ambulance' – 'I can't say it,' and when I demonstrated, he repeated it correctly after me.

Overheard while he was playing with blocks, with Mama as audience: 'The bear is riding on the train, and everyone is *astonished*' (slowly and with emphasis) 'to see that bear riding on the train.'

Last night Erwin did the main work of putting Daniel to bed. He told me that Daniel got very cross and threw all the bears on the floor.

Erwin said, 'I know you're sad because Sarah isn't here. But it won't bring her back if you throw the bears on the floor. We are all sad because she isn't here. We all want her back very much.'

As soon as he said this, Daniel's rage stopped and he listened gravely.

Erwin said, 'I'll lie down on Sarah's bed while you go to sleep so that you won't be by yourself. I know I'm not Sarah, but you will have someone with you.'

Daniel wanted to lie on Sarah's bed too, and Erwin suggested that they lie there together until Daniel went to sleep and then Erwin would put him back into his cot.

Daniel, 'I want to get into Sarah's bed.'

They came into our room where I was sitting on the bed reading.

Erwin said, 'Daniel has an idea he wants to tell you.'

Daniel held Erwin's hand, and looked very grave and grown-up and handsome. They told me of their proposal that Daniel should sleep in Sarah's bed, and I agreed it was a good idea, and went and got sheets, made the bed, put two bears and the kangaroo in it, and then Erwin and I put Daniel to bed, and Erwin sat with him till he went to sleep.

June 30
Daniel, this afternoon, 'I want to see Sarah.'

After dinner, building a high tower with blocks: 'One day Sarah will come and see the tower we're building.'

July 1

Daniel, this morning on my knee in the kitchen: 'Talk to me about Sarah.'

'What would you like me to tell you about?'

'Tell me about the beginning.'

So I told a story which I had never before told for him alone, though he had often overheard me telling Sarah, because it had been a favourite of hers.

'Once, a long while ago, before you were born, Mummy and Daddy didn't have any children. They thought it would be lovely to have a little baby, so they started to grow one. It grew in Mummy's tummy and it was so tiny to start with that you would hardly have been able to see it. And it grew to be this big, and then it grew to be this big, and when it was about this big it was time for it to come out into the world. That is called being born. And Mummy went to hospital for the baby to be born, because after a baby is born you feel rather tired and it is nice to rest in bed. And then that baby was born, and the doctor said, "It's a girl!" because before the baby is born no one knows whether it is a boy or a girl. And the doctor rang up Daddy and said, "You've got a daughter," and Daddy suddenly felt very happy. And a bit later he came to see Mummy in hospital, and nursed the baby Sarah. And it had been raining very hard when Mummy went to hospital, but when Sarah was born the sun came out. And a week after Sarah was born, we both went for a walk in Regent's Park with Sarah, and all the tulips were out, the most wonderful colours shining in the sun.'

'I remember it all exactly,' Erwin commented.

This is what I told Daniel today, but the story has been told many times with many variations of detail.

July 2

Ruth was due to return to New York today. Several times while Erwin and I were talking to her after breakfast Daniel asked, 'Are you talking about Sarah?' On the way to the airport, as we turned into Flemington Road near the Children's Hospital, 'Are we going to see Sarah?' Both the children had keen memories for roads and often, driving along some stretch of road, they would recall our destination on some previous occasion when we had driven there.

July 4

Several times today Daniel insisted that he was not Daniel, or any other name, but Feddy-puss. Also, slightly worried, he said several times, 'Don't let anything come and get me.' And 'I want Sarah to be here,' and 'Sometimes Sarah called the kitten Blackie.' (Its usual name was Kim, a name also given by her.)

'Feddy-puss' refers to an incident perhaps six weeks ago. I had gone out into the garden and seen the two of them playing together on the grass near the old washhouse. As I went up to them, they presented themselves side by side before me, like actors in front of the curtain.

Sarah waved a hand towards Daniel and introduced him: 'This is Feddy, my puss-cat. He's a nice little cat. He doesn't scratch or bite.'

Daniel screwed up his face in a feline smirk and looked very pleased.

July 5

When we visited the Traills a few days ago, Daniel was rather grizzly and fretful. While he was out of the room visiting the cat with Ed, I said to Maggie, 'Of course he's still very upset.'

'Yes,' she replied dubiously. 'And I suppose he's got a bit spoiled, with everyone fussing over him.'

The fear of giving children too much, whether of attention or things! Children as having boundless greed – as soon as you cease regularly to deny them, they will become quite insatiable and unreasonable in their demands. That this can be seen as the dominant process even so soon after a terrible bereavement. The implication is that even in these circumstances, if he had been fussed over less he wouldn't grizzle so much. Well, she could even be right. But it seems to me that in these circumstances he has a much greater need than usual to be comforted and loved and reassured.

Tonight Daniel announced firmly at dinner to Mama, 'I'm Dr Poss.'

Sarah used to play at being Dr Poss with Mama, especially in her bedroom in the morning. Erwin and I had already complained to each other that the content of this game was lost – all Mama could say was that she used to play it for hours. But now we learned a little.

Daniel, tonight: 'I'm going to give you a hard injection. It's going to hurt a little . . . No, it's not going to hurt. Then I'll give you a toffee. And I'm going to put some cream on your finger, and a Bandaid.'

But after taking over her role like this, as we were going upstairs, he said, 'I wish Sarah were here!' and 'Once Sarah came upstairs with a blue thing on.'

At bedtime I read a story in which there is a reference to billy tea.

Daniel: 'Once we had a billy of tea.'

'Yes, we had a billy of tea several times. Once was the last time we went away on a trip. We had a picnic at a crossroads. Do you remember? You and Sarah wanted to cross the road.'

'Yes, Sarah wanted to see the house.' (True. This was on May 9.)

July 6

I thought Daniel was beginning to recover and look happier and be more of the time absorbed in other things, but much of today has been filled with terrible rage and dissatisfaction. Didn't want to go to Mama's lavatory, but to Daddy's. Then not to Daddy's but to the outside one. Wanted to go to feed the swans – yells and tears when we said it was too late.

I had a long talk with him, telling him that it really wouldn't help to go to the outside lavatory rather than the inside one – that wouldn't bring Sarah back. And about how much we all wanted her back and had all tried to help her get better; even the ambulance men had only wanted to get her to hospital to be made better.

He looked solemn and said, 'Tell me about Sarah.'

I asked whether he wanted to know what happened to Sarah, or about how she played with him. He asked to be told about how they played together, and laughed and cheered up when I talked of their games of chasey in the garden when it was time for his rest.

This calmed him for a while, but now, by evening, he is again fractious, and bad-tempered and crying. Apart from his grief, he has really not learned, like an only child, to play alone for long hours.

Earlier in the day he said, 'Show me a book with a picture of Sarah.'

'I'll show you some photographs of Sarah. There's a lovely one on Grandpa's mantelpiece, of Sarah when she was a lot younger.'

'I'd like a mantelpiece with a picture of Sarah.'

From time to time, over several days, he has said, rather

33

softly but crossly, 'I don't want Sarah back,' 'I don't want Sarah to be here.' Also, repeatedly, 'I'm not anything,' when asked that favourite question, who are you?

July 7

At bedtime Daniel wanted 'Pat-a-cake', but before I sang it he asked that it should be put in the oven for the swans and ducks. We sang various and increasingly long versions of this, for the swans with red beaks, and the cygnets, and the seagulls and the sparrows – all birds we fed this afternoon and on other days. Then he asked for 'all the animals in the zoo'. I said, wouldn't we have one for 'Sarah and me', as we have had the other nights.

Daniel: 'No. For the swans and the ducks and all the animals.'

July 8

Erwin and I commented this afternoon that Daniel looked much better today. Beverly [*Sarah's favourite nurse, who had just returned from her honeymoon*] was back for the first time, and Dan helped her hang the washing out, handing her the pegs, as Sarah used to but he had never done before. Erwin and I went into town, and Dan waved goodbye quite cheerfully. He went with Grandpa and Beverly and Mama to the gardens to feed the swans, and when we got back from town he was playing with the tractors and seemed absorbed. He helped Erwin make carrot salad for dinner – Erwin grated the carrot and Daniel was the crane which lifted it into the bowl.

But during dinner he was restless and noisy and not hungry, and kept wanting to play too roughly with the cat. Then he did and didn't want to wee.

Finally he said, 'I want Sarah.'

'I do too, darling.'

'Can't we go and get Sarah back?'

'No we can't. Sarah's gone a long way away, off with the angels, and we can't get her back. Sarah died. She was killed by germs.'

I try to explain germs, that they are tiny little animals too small to see without a special machine.

'Sarah's heart stopped.'

'Yes it did. The germs made her so very sick that her heart stopped.'

'I want to torture old Dad.'

So I talked about how the two of them used to play 'Let's torture old Dad.' It was a way of working off that nervous energy which is part tiredness and part boredom, in the evening, or when we were returning from a long drive in the country. They would climb on him, ruffle his hair, pull his ears, tumble from his shoulders, tug at his clothes – a cheerful roughing-up that verged on the sadistic. As he listened, Daniel's face lit up, and he added details – 'And I hit him in the face.' Then I talked about how they played bears and everyone laughed, and Dad crawled up and down the floor with Sarah and Daniel on his back, and they both shrieked.

'And I whacked him,' Daniel added.

July 9

As I was putting him to bed, Daniel reminded me that he wanted a picture of Sarah on his mantelpiece. So I asked him if he would like the one from Grandpa's mantelpiece until he got one of his own. He said yes, and we took it upstairs, Daniel rather grave. He insisted on carrying the photograph into the bathroom so that I could hold him up to the mirror and he could see himself and Sarah reflected together.

Paul and Erwin talked last night about what we had told Daniel and how much he understood. Paul recommended that we tell Daniel a story, such as that Sarah had gone away for a holiday.

Erwin said, 'Well what good would it do to tell him that, seeing that he saw Sarah drive off in the ambulance?' (He could have added 'and seeing that he saw Sarah's dead body.')

Paul replied that we were intellectualising too much, that children don't understand all that clearly, and he still maintained that we should spin a story. Odd that Paul, an intellectual himself if ever there was one, should make this complaint. But I don't think that the way we talk to Daniel stems from intellectualising, even though we accept an occasional hint from Cecily. It comes from the empathic conviction that he feels as we do, the same longings and contradictions and struggles to believe the incredible.

Daniel invented a new game which he never played with Sarah, a game of 'tennis' using wooden blocks for both racket and ball. But Sarah was still in his mind. While playing he said, 'Hey, look at my little puss-face,' screwing up his face as he used to when playing Feddy-puss with Sarah.

July 12

Daniel looks very pale and stricken still, except when there is something special to absorb his attention. He spent two hours at the Burnstocks and they said he enjoyed it, but when he saw me at the door he stretched out his arms and said he wanted to go home. When we got here, he said, 'Our Sarah's upstairs' – meaning the photograph. But as we climbed the stairs, 'I wish the real Sarah was here.' I think his desperation increases in the same way and for the same reason that ours does – that it gets more certainly borne in on him that he mustn't expect to see her again. He hasn't said for a while 'Let's go and get her back.'

During the weekend he said, 'The children's hospital is a long way away.'

'No, it's not such a long way, but Sarah isn't there now. She died, and then suddenly our Sarah wasn't there any more. Only her body was left behind, and without Sarah that wasn't any use.'

A frequent question lately: 'Are the angels up in the snow?'

I reply that I don't think so. I think they are much further away, where no one can go.

July 14
A screaming fit while we were doing the shopping. A sour elderly lady looked disapprovingly at us, and I almost said to her, 'He's got a good reason for crying – his sister has died.'

July 15
The continuing use of grandparents. Daniel the last two mornings has had long and cheerful sessions in Mama's room while she finishes her breakfast.

July 20
It is difficult to get Daniel to take enough exercise now that he is alone. He tries riding his bike, but half a turn round the drive is enough. When Sarah was playing in the garden he would keep it up for a long time even if she were not riding, but just in the garden with him. This afternoon I played trains, choofing round the drive in the opposite

direction to him on his bike. He enjoyed that, and I was the one to stop. I remember that about eighteen months ago, when Daniel was not yet a companion for her, Sarah would only stay in the garden when an adult was there, and I used to do extra gardening jobs to encourage her to be outside. This evening we had a bit of a game of chasey, but it is very different. Sarah and Daniel together would keep it up for a long time with only the slightest encouragement from Erwin or me. They were so quick and lively, and got so excited, and wriggled so fiercely if caught, that it seemed, even though the adults were not seriously contending, like a real contest. Daniel used to run more easily into traps than Sarah, but he wriggled out of them furiously. We all loved the game. I remember describing it to Laurie O'Brien, and she remarked on how much easier it is to amuse two than one.

Tonight it needed continual effort from both Erwin and me to keep up enough spirit and excitement. Daniel appeared to quite enjoy it, but to us it seemed a very forced performance. Active involvement always did get boring – that is why it used to be so marvellous to set the two of them going and then watch them keep it up for themselves. Daniel tonight trotted and squeaked in something of the old way, but he was too easily caught and didn't fight to free himself, so I had to make only the slightest gesture of catching him and then send him on his way.

July 22

Daniel hasn't mentioned the hope of seeing Sarah again for several weeks. But this morning Erwin gave him a banana and then took him out in the car.

He said, 'When I'm three I'm going to school, and then Sarah will come back from the angels and we'll have lots and lots of bananas and pears and apples to take to school in our paper bags, and we'll go to school together.'

Constant realisation of the truth is too terrible for him. We don't encourage the hope of seeing her again; we have said she won't be coming back, and if he asks us again whether she will come back, we say no. But I don't think I could take a positive step to destroy this fantasy when he puts it forward.

In the evening I learned the source of his renewed hopefulness. On going to bed, Daniel asked me to sing the song I sang last night. I didn't understand which song he meant, until he said, 'About the angels coming.' I remembered then that the previous night I had sung 'Swing Low, Sweet Chariot' at Daniel's request. He had learned it from Grandpa during the afternoon. He had fastened on the words 'A band of angels coming after me, Coming for to carry me home.' Tonight he made me repeat the song about six times. Once he said, 'Those are the angels that look after you when you're sick.' And now I remember that this morning was the first time he has woken up to find that I had already gone downstairs without starting to cry. He called out and I went up immediately, as I always do. He was standing at the top of the stairs looking cheerful. On previous occasions he had been sitting on the bed in tears.

July 24
Since 'Swing Low', Daniel talks more freely about Sarah. Yesterday he saw in Erwin's room a little drawing of a white bird on red paper and asked what it was. Erwin said it had been the wrapper of one of Sarah's Christmas presents. Daniel seemed to like it, and Erwin suggested they pin it up in the playroom. Daniel helped, and said, 'Sarah will be pleased to see it when she comes home.'

Today, returning from shopping in the car, I said, using the word we had invented for the children when they were being uncooperative, 'You're a tired boggs, aren't you?'

'I'm not a boggs.'

'What are you?'

'I'm Sarah's Feddy.'

'You're Sarah's Feddy-puss?'

'No, I'm not Feddy-puss. I'm just Sarah's Feddy.'

July 28

Daniel: 'Sarah used to say, "Look Daniel, there's a tractor."'

To me: 'Are the angels going to make Sarah better?'

'No darling. Our beautiful Sarah was so ill that the angels couldn't make her better.'

I discussed my answer afterwards with Erwin, who thought I had been a bit too severe. But it doesn't seem to have left too great a shadow – his spirits and energy improve, and I don't think he now has cross spells more often than before she died.

July 29

Daniel was very lively last night. He made puss faces and puss hisses in the bathroom when I wanted to clean his teeth, and played a repetitive laughing game – all I had to do each time was open my eyes very wide and he laughed. In the bedroom he said he wanted to dance; he leaped around like Sarah in what she called 'doing Ladies', then held my hand and we danced in a ring. I read a story and he had a session of tumbling and laughter with Erwin. After all that he came downstairs again and played quietly for half an hour, so determined not to go to bed that I let him stay. When I took him up again, he asked me to sing to him.

He still didn't want to go to bed, but had become rather solemn, and finally I said, 'You miss Sarah, don't you?'

He said 'Yes', and I talked for a while about how if she were here they would play chasey and laugh together, and then he would sleep in the cot and Sarah in her bed. As soon as I talked of her he became calm, as if an enormous weight had been lifted from his stomach; he crawled into bed, lay down, and was soon asleep.

Although I know by now how much all this is constantly in his mind, and how clear are the meanings of play and stories, it was only this morning that I saw the connection between last night's dancing and a story he had asked for repeatedly through the day – the story of Tico-tico the squirrel, who falls in love with a girl-cat and wants to stay with her. She is disdainful and he can do nothing to please her until she sees him dance. Then they both dance together. This morning he asked, first thing, for Tico-tico again.

I read it and then said, 'They danced together like Sarah and Daniel, didn't they?'

Daniel smiled very happily and said, 'Yes.'

July 31
Sarah's most terrible experience was my operation and subsequent period of illness. She wanted to hear the story endless times, and it must have been the source of those games of playing sick and hospitals, and of her fear of hospital on the day of her death. Yet the story of my operation had a happy ending. There was some reassurance to be drawn from hearing it, because I was with her to tell it.

Daniel's most terrible experience is Sarah's death, and in this there is no reassurance and no happy ending. We add a bit of comfort in the story about the angels, but it is a very limited consolation. I can't add much convincing detail, my heart isn't in it, and the real reassurance, which would be her return or even my promising that she will return, is something I can't give. I don't even feel the angels story will stand for much repetition, and I also feel it isn't enough. Last night at bedtime he looked solemn and as if waiting for something. I didn't feel I had anything to give.

August 2

Today while I was dressing, Daniel said, 'The doors of the hospital where Sarah was opened by themselves.' Then he added, reflectively, 'Did Sarah's heart stop beating?'

'Yes, Sarah's heart stopped beating because she was so very sick, and she died.'

'Before she died, did her heart beat?'

'Yes, her heart beat all the time. Everyone's heart beats all the time – yours and mine and Daddy's.'

'Did the angels come here to get Sarah?'

'No, we took her to hospital and that is where she died, and the angels took her from there. We took her to hospital because we thought that the doctors could make her better, but she was too sick.'

After this conversation he went up to Erwin in the kitchen and said he wanted to listen to his heart beat.

August 7

I have sung 'Swing Low, Sweet Chariot' to Daniel at bedtime almost every night for several weeks. He also often asks for 'The Red Flag', obviously relishing its talk of blood and death. I had to ring up Geoff Hutton to complete my knowledge of the words.

August 11

I have recently introduced into the story of the angels the notion of heaven and earth. 'Sarah can't be here because people who go to heaven can't come back.' I thought when he kept asking if the angels had made Sarah better, that the notion that we don't know much about what it is like to be with the angels is too much like the notion that Sarah doesn't exist any more, and he is too young to have to bear such a black thought. And for some reason I said that the rest of us were on earth. That must be hard to understand, since the earth is everything he sees. He asked me yesterday, 'Who is on earth?', and when I said we all were he didn't look as though he understood.

August 13

Last night as I was putting him to bed he said, positively and quite cheerfully, 'Sarah's here. She's downstairs.'

'Where is she?' I asked.

'In the playroom.'

'What is she doing?'

'She's brushing fluff off her dress.'

August 20

Daniel: 'Not many people die, do they?'

'No, not many people. Young people don't often die. Old people die.'

'The angels take old people. But first they go to hospital.'

'Sometimes they go to hospital but not always. Sometimes the angels come and take them from home.'

I told him about Grandma Gray, who died at home when he was ten months old. 'But most people who go to hospital don't die, they go to be made better. Do you know who is in hospital right now? David.' And I talked about David's broken leg and how it would be in plaster for a long time, and Daniel would see him when he came home.

This was about an hour ago. Now Daniel is in the next room, building a hospital with blocks, 'with rooms for all the boys and girls, and three resting rooms. And I'm going to put Sarah in that hospital. It's a hospital for Sarah.'

August 22

I took Daniel with me when I went to the dentist. He must have remembered going there with Sarah because in the waiting room he said, 'I want to see Sarah.' While I was in the dentist's chair, Dr French looked at Daniel and said, 'Who is he like?'

'He's like both of us,' I replied, adding, since Daniel was there, 'You look like Mummy and like Daddy, don't you?'

Daniel: 'I look like our Sarah.'

Dr French: 'He hasn't forgotten her.'

'Why should he?' I asked, and his comment was, 'In time, nothing will remain but a happy memory.'

Like most people, he wants to deny or minimise Daniel's grief. But I think sadness will remain with him always, alongside happy memories. Like the child survivors of Hiroshima in *Children of the A-Bomb* who, six years later, thought sadly of their little dead sister all the time.

Cecily de Monchaux flew out to Sydney during the long vacation and paid us a visit of several days. Her company was an immense solace. She was the only friend with whom we were able to talk freely and naturally about the events of Sarah's death and our own reactions. Referring to Daniel's way of coping, she used a phrase which seemed

44

*particularly apt, and which I often thought of after she had gone –
'the flight to reality'. I don't know whether it is an established
psychoanalytic term or whether she invented it for the occasion. I
have never seen it used anywhere else, nor am I sure precisely what it
means. I suppose she must have meant flight from unconscious
fantasies of guilt and threat, of attacking and being attacked. To me
it meant rather flight from the powerful emotions of outrage and
disbelief that surged up again and again in manifold shifting forms,
however firmly and rationally I tried to control them. I don't know
whether Daniel felt that persistent sense of injustice, but for him as
for all of us there is unfathomable mystery in the contrast between
life and death, and in the waywardness with which death strikes.
Physical facts by contrast have a comforting hardness and stability,
and it was certainly to them that Daniel turned. It was under his
persistent pressure that I gradually told him more about Sarah's
illness and death, and eventually about the disposal of her body. In
later conversations he responded with boredom, puzzlement or scorn
to explanations that invoked sorrow, or enduring love, or the
consolations of memory.*

*I can apply the concept of the flight to reality to myself also. I
found solace there too: in the reality of putting words on paper; in
striving to make those words an accurate record; in talking to Daniel
about the physical reality of sickness and death, instead of giving
way in solitude to longing and despair.*

September 1
This morning while I was making the beds, Daniel said,
'If Sarah were here we would say "Let's torture old Dad,
he doesn't mind!" and we would all be happy. But if I do
an emu dance, we are not happy.'

I said that we loved to see him do his emu dance, and it
made us very happy. He does it very well, poking his head
forward and making throaty emu noises.

This afternoon, to me: 'Did your heart stop? . . . Sarah's

heart only stopped for a little while, then it started going again . . . Sarah's in the playroom . . . You're Sarah.'

September 3

A boy's love of women is said to be a transformation of his love for his mother, but I wonder whether it may not in some cases be an overflow and transformation of love for a sister. Since the day last November, when he was two years and three months old, when Sarah first invited some girls from the nursery school home to play, Daniel has always been attracted by little girls, is happy to see them, and shows off in their presence. Since Sarah died, it is the girls among the children we have arranged for him to see who move him. E.g., on the way home from shopping, I suggested we call on Sam.

Dan said, 'No, let's call on Noni.'

He wants songs sung at bedtime about Tammy and Viva, Noni, Margaret, but he has never asked for a song about any of the boys. Tammy, the first of these new loves, looks a bit like Sarah, and we commented on it the first time we saw her. Daniel repeated several times, 'She looks a bit like Sarah.'

September 4

While I was dressing Daniel, he said, 'I wish Sarah was here to ride her bike round the drive. She used to say "Time to turn round!"'

Most of his talk about Sarah now takes this form of accurate and wistful memory, though sometimes he still talks hopefully of her return. But although he is often sadly conscious of her absence, he doesn't seem to be as unceasingly aware of it as we are. He plays, very gaily and with tremendous energy, animal and hiding games that

46

have evolved since she died into something quite different from anything he played with her. I repeated to Erwin his remark about wishing Sarah were here to ride her bike.

Erwin: 'How very mature that is. It makes me furious to think of Paul wanting us to tell him ridiculous lies.'

Later, while I was shopping in Dickins, I thought that if Daniel is adult in his ability to accept and remember, I am like a child in my recurrent inability to believe. I think, fleetingly but often, something like, 'Sarah is so full of energy, or love, or inventiveness, that she can't be dead. She isn't dead. We will see her again.' It's not quite as definite as that. A feeling and a vision of Sarah alive, that disappears as soon as I look at it or try to put it into words. I am like four-year-old Peter, described by Dorothy Burlingham and Anna Freud: 'My Daddy is killed, yes, my sister said so. He cannot come. I want him to come. My Daddy is big, he can do everything.'

Freud said that no one believes in his or her own death, but I discover now that one cannot believe in the death of someone one truly loves. Not if they are young; perhaps when they have already passed the peak of life and are going downward, perhaps then one would believe.

September 5
Daniel, playing in the tent we have made out of rugs in the playroom: 'That's my door, and that's Sarah's door. Only Sarah's not here, so she can't peep out of her door.'

That night Daniel insisted on going to sleep in the tent instead of being taken up to bed. He got out to fetch his horsey pillow and went to sleep with it under his head. The horsey pillow was given to him at the same time as Sarah got her piggy pillow, but whereas she always slept with hers, he wasn't previously much interested in his.

47

September 7

Sometimes his fantasy about Sarah's presence is fully conscious. When we came downstairs this morning he said, 'Let's pretend our Sarah's here.'

So I talked about how Sarah would say, 'Is it time for me to go down to the gate and wait for Beverly?'

'And she would say "Where's my Feddy-puss?"'

'And then you'd all come up the drive together, talking.'

Yesterday he asked: 'Have the angels made Sarah better?'

'Yes, the angels have made Sarah better so that she isn't sick any more, but they haven't made her so that she can come back to us, because when you die you can't come back again.'

I added another detail to the angel fantasy last week. I'm not sure that I was right; I try to avoid adding embroidery. We were about to read a favourite story of Sarah's and I said, (prompted, I think, by a remark of Daniel's), 'I think perhaps Sarah might be able to hear us. We can't see her, but perhaps she can hear us. So we'll read the story for Sarah and Daniel.' He liked this idea, and has referred to it several times since.

Just now he came to me and said, cheerfully, 'Hey, I'm Daniel and you're Sarah . . . We're going to pretend that you're Sarah.'

September 8

We have made a sudden decision to go to Sydney, as a break, and to see Cecily again before she returns to London. Daniel has heard us talk about the trip, and a few days ago got very upset and cried, 'I don't want to go to Sydney.'

I talked to him about Cecily, and her nephews and nieces, and the zoo and the beach, and said we would only be gone for about a week and then we would come back. He was reassured, and said quite boastfully and cheerfully to Mama and Grandpa, 'We're going to Sydney.'

The trip to Sydney was almost the first time we had been out of Melbourne since Sarah's death. Not quite the first; we had earlier attempted a country excursion of the kind that once used to be an intense pleasure for us all, exploring back roads and unfamiliar places, stopping often to walk in the bush, or to picnic, or to explore a timber-mill in its silent Sunday abandonment. I didn't at first understand, after she died, that these outings had suddenly become impossible, and on one early Sunday I had planned a trip to an abandoned mining town, the sort of place we had previously particularly enjoyed. It was a ghastly, painful, endless day, saturated with awareness of her absence. Not until a year later, on the first anniversary of her death, did I dare to try again.

The journey to Sydney by car was not planned as an immersion in the Australian countryside, but encounters with its splendour were unavoidable. Once more I stared from an immense distance, isolated by pain, seeing every place as a place where Sarah was not and would never be. I recall with a particularly lurid sense of unreality a halt near Goulburn, that 'City of Lilacs' where a year earlier the four of us had tumbled out of the car in golden evening light to refresh ourselves after a long drive. This time we looked for a picnic place that might please Daniel, and found one that was perfect, where a track curved down to a creek with a little sandy beach and a plank bridge from which sticks could be dropped into the water. The air was sweet, the sun warm, and the hillsides covered with a pale gold blaze of wattle. I felt a certain satisfaction at noting that my talent for reading the signs was still working, but beyond that only a cold indifference to so much characteristic Australian beauty. Daniel's play by the creek, too, was listless.

In Sydney, thinking to avoid the poignant memories associated with the Rushcutters' Bay Motel where we had stayed the year before with Sarah, I had booked a room in a motel in Manly, but it seemed so far away and forlorn that after one night we moved back to Rushcutters'. There was a certain solace in its familiarity and efficient modernity.

I had brought a typewriter with me, and while Daniel had his afternoon sleep I wrote, more to continue exploring my own grief than to record events of the trip. The only notes about Daniel are the two entries which follow.

September 9

A sunny morning in Gundagai after our first night away from home without Sarah. Daniel asked, 'Is Sarah going to Sydney?'

'No darling, but we all went to Sydney last year. We stayed in a motel with a swimming pool and you and Sarah had a room to yourselves. Do you remember?'

'Sarah and I had a room to ourselves at Peterborough.' [*This had been a rare event.*] 'Sarah said, "Where's Mr Peterborough?" and I said, "Where's Mr Kookaburra?" and we both laughed. Sarah said, "Where's Mr Peterborough?" and I said, "Mr Kookaburra?"' He spoke in an exaggerated mock-satirical tone.

Daniel laughed very cheerfully while he said this. To remember Sarah at that moment seemed to be pure joy. I think this is possible for him because he has no conception of the immensity of the future during which we won't see Sarah. He can miss her in the present, or remember her happily in the past, but he has no premonition of the vast empty future which will never be made joyful by her companionship.

September 10

Daniel has played throughout the trip at being Sarah *and* Daniel. Soon after we left Melbourne he knelt up in the back seat and began chanting, as they used to together, 'Faster! Faster!' He said, 'I'm Sarah calling out Faster, Faster, and this is Daniel calling out Faster, Faster' – indicating the seat beside him.

Last night, going down the stairs in the Manly motel he said, 'Sarah's going downstairs in front and Daniel's going downstairs behind.'
   'Sarah's in front of you, is she darling?'
   Daniel: 'No, I'm Sarah.'
   In the car he has repeatedly said something like this: 'Sarah's showing Daniel the ships. Look Daniel, there are the ships. Sarah shows Daniel the ships because Daniel likes ships.' And: 'Sarah says, Look, Daniel, there's a tractor. Because tractors and trucks are instrutting, but cars aren't instrutting.'

At Rushcutters' Bay, Daniel had a cot in our room, in which he could fall asleep to the sound of our talk with friends over steaks sent down from the restaurant. We spent rewarding days with Cecily and with her family and friends. By the end of the week we had gained enough courage to choose an unfamiliar route for the return journey, and this time Nature echoed our inner preoccupations by providing settings of appropriate strangeness and discomfort – shrouding the cliffs at Katoomba in thick mist, freezing the night air to piercing sharpness as we wandered along the deserted main street of Bathurst gazing at window-displays, and giving us a midday picnic site next day in a featureless patch of bush studded with rainwater puddles.

On the last night of the journey home, we stopped for supper after night had fallen, while we were still a long way from home, turning off the highway down an anonymous dirt track. For some reason we had a chop picnic. It was again a cold night, and very dark, with the starry Australian sky glittering high above us but giving no light; the three of us stood in a circle of firelight surrounded by infinite silent darkness. I think it was the first time that I was aware that we were becoming a new entity, bound together by our common experience as survivors and able to find pleasure together, even though subdued and melancholy. The knowledge was not fully conscious, and not yet a reliable source of strength, but I remember thinking that the fragment of time, in a place whose precise location I would never know, had an austere beauty that was somehow acceptable and consoling.

September 24

Since we returned from Sydney, Daniel has much less often played at being Sarah. He sometimes calls himself Sarah, or Sarah Roberta Penny (Roberta and Penny being two little girls we met in Sydney), or when I call him boykin or boyo, says he isn't boykin, he's a girl. A few times on going to the lavatory he has said, 'I'm not a boy; I haven't got a penis' – but playfully and entirely without distress. But he hasn't so often played games in which Sarah and Daniel are said to be both participating.

On the other hand he has remembered her sadly and directly more often. When he saw Betty [*my sister*] for the first time since our return, he said, 'I miss Sarah.' He has said the same thing to both Erwin and me at night when he couldn't sleep. After we have talked about her, he has settled down.

October 5

Daniel yesterday morning: 'I wish the Sarah-swan was here.'

Sarah is often a swan in his fantasy. In the weeks after she died we went almost every day to feed the swans in the Botanical Gardens. We bought him a story-book about a swan, and for weeks it was almost the only story he wanted. Sarah had an inflatable swan beach toy, which still hangs in the garage. Daniel has several times asked to have it down to play with, and only a few days ago as I drove into the garage, he said, 'That's Sarah's swan.'

For Erwin and me also the swan has symbolised the paradise when Sarah was alive. Last summer she used to leave it in the canvas paddling pool on the back lawn, under the dappled shade of a plum tree, and we could see it from our windows, swimming serenely round in the breeze, a gay and reassuring token of her presence.

Another source of the swan fantasy is, I think, wings – the huge wings of the swan are like the wings of the angels who have carried Sarah far away. And there is also whiteness, the whiteness of some swans – not the black Australian swans in the Botanical Gardens, but the white swans in his book and in England, a long way away. And the whiteness of the snow-mountains which are also high up and a long way away.

Daniel has asked several times, 'Is Sarah in the snow? Is she at Mount Buller?' and I have said, 'No, she is much further away than that; she is somewhere where no one can go.'

But I think he still pictures her somewhere among far-off snowy mountains. He was happy to see the snow-covered mountains, looking distant and unattainable, from the highway to Sydney. He talked of them for days, and built snow-mountains in the sand. Now he paints snow with white paint on a sheet of cardboard in Erwin's studio.

He still often says 'I'm Sarah and this is Daniel,' looking at a space about a foot away from himself. I remembered this morning that this phrase was one Sarah often used when asked her name by strangers.

November 10

Yesterday evening Erwin burned his arm when he unstoppered the car radiator and a mixture of boiling water and oil fountained out. I took him to St Vincent's Hospital to have it dressed, and Daniel came too. In the car on the way he asked, without any apparent terror, 'Is Daddy going to die?' Waiting at the hospital while Erwin had his arm dressed, he asked, 'Why can't Sarah come back?'

A patient on a stretcher was wheeled past the end of the corridor. I said that he was very sick and had been brought in an ambulance. Daniel wanted to see him, but I said he would already have gone upstairs in the lift.

Daniel: 'Is he choking?'

When we left, there was an ambulance in the forecourt. Daniel: 'That's the ambulance Sarah went in.'

Many times when we have talked of sick people and of death he has said, 'Sarah had flu, that's why she died,' and I have tried to explain that not everyone who has flu dies, that it only happens to a rare and unlucky person. Yesterday he said, 'Jamie and Alastair are boys. That's why they won't die.' Jamie and Alastair have flu.

I have told him the full story of Sarah's illness and death only once or twice, in the first weeks after she died, but he remembers every single detail and has recalled one or another of them on different occasions.

'Sarah's heart stopped beating!'

'Did Sarah leave her body behind?'

November 12

Daniel: 'Sarah said to the cat, "You mustn't swallow the marble, that's not at all good for you."'

November 19
In the past few weeks Daniel has been anxious about going any great distance away from home. He asks when we go out, 'Is it very far? I don't want to go there. Will we be able to come home?' Yesterday I said that one day we would go to Paris together. Daniel asked, 'Is Paris a long way away? Can you get back from Paris?'

'Was Uncle Bruce an old man when he died?'
  I have said from time to time that most people don't die until they are very old. I want to try to convince him that a sudden young death like Sarah's is rare. I don't want him to be thinking that he himself, or one of us, is likely to die at any moment. [*But my brother Bruce was yet another person who died suddenly, and relatively young.*]

November 20
A few days ago Daniel announced, 'Once Sarah and I played with starfish.'
  This morning he recalled that he and Sarah had watched starfish on the beach near Lorne. He said, as if absent-mindedly, 'If you turn the starfish over, do you die?'
  I assured him no.
  There was a pause and then, cuddling up to me, he said, 'I'm unhappy without my Sarah.'
  A little later he asked me again, 'Why did Sarah die?'
  I talked once more about her illness, but I had to explain that lots of boys and girls and grown-ups get flu, and they nearly all get better again; that Sarah was very very ill; and that we just don't know why she was so ill that she died. I don't see how it can be other than a tremendous puzzle, and why all sorts of possibilities should not present themselves to him.

He has asked a number of times, 'When Sarah took her temperature in her mouth, did she die?' – because it was unusual for her to take the thermometer in her mouth; both of them disliked it.

November 28
Daniel asked me a few days ago, 'When did Sarah die?'
I said in June.
'And before that was she alive?'
Yesterday, 'I wish Sarah hadn't died in June,' and later, 'Could Noni be our Sarah?'
I said that Noni had her own mummy and daddy, and that besides no one could be our own lovely Sarah, there was only one Sarah and she was dead.
Daniel: 'No, there isn't only one Sarah, there's Sarah Littlejohn.'
When I replied, 'Yes, that's true, there's quite a lot of little girls called Sarah', he looked very cheerful.

He asked me, 'Where's Sarah's bear now?'
I said it was in the cupboard in Erwin's room.
'You remember when we went to see Sarah in the hospital after she had died, she was lying in bed with the bear beside her. After that, Daddy brought it home.'
'Yes, and she had a book about Monkey beside her.'
I am sure no one has recalled this to him during the five and a half months since she died.

When we saw Betty's swimming-pool for the first time this season, a few days ago: 'Sarah used to swim in the pool. She used to swim like a fish.' (Sarah had been fond of this phrase, and used it to describe her own prowess.)

December 2
Daniel now talks a great deal about Sarah, and most of it is very specific and accurately remembered. E.g., he said to Erwin this morning, 'Sarah had jelly beans when it was time for her to die,' and to me, 'Sarah had a shower once.'

When we are picking out letters, S is always for Sarah. He sat on my knee at the typewriter yesterday, and when I suggested we type a word, he said, 'Write Sarah!' To talk about her comforts and pleases him and he often smiles happily.

On Sunday I overheard him telling Viva and Tammy, 'My Sarah had flu.'

December 4
We had been talking about relationships.
    'And if we adopt a little baby girl, she will be your sister,' I said.
    'Can she be my own sister Sarah?'

This oblique note is the first reference in the diary to the possibility that we might adopt a baby, although we had been thinking about it. I recall talking to Cecily when she visited us in September. For Erwin and me it was a profound issue, but we would not have discussed it in front of Daniel.
    I was aware at every moment of the irreversibility of Sarah's death. A unique individual had gone, but our lives had also changed in ways that seemed almost impersonal. The house had become forlornly empty.
    'I feel as though our family has been reduced not by a quarter but to a quarter,' Erwin said.
    I too contemplated the change in mathematical terms, those of a minor branch of social science whose geometrical diagrams suddenly

57

took on a cogency they had never had before. Within a family of four, I calculated, eleven small societies are constantly forming, disappearing and reappearing, as the quadrilateral of two parents and two children divides to form any of four possible triangles and six possible dyads. Each of these figures had a distinct emotional atmosphere, and its own evolving traditions, pleasures and disciplines. I could picture Sarah flirtatious with Erwin, serious with me, protectively condescending with Daniel; the two children alone with their father were wilder and gayer than with their responsible and practical mother; and so on. Eleven constellations in a family of four, but only four in a family of three.

This drastic reduction of possibility would continue after grief had faded. But if we had another child, the richness of variation would be restored. I couldn't have another baby of my own, but perhaps we could adopt one. Soon I believed that it was what we should do, although Erwin was never whole-heartedly convinced, and supported the idea only because I appeared to want it so badly.

The new baby would have to be a girl because one of the qualities I yearned to restore to our life was femininity: prettiness, vanity, flirtatiousness, excitement about clothes and other decorative frivolities, eager involvement with people and tenderhearted concern for them, flattering attentiveness, ready kisses and eager embraces. Even more than femininity, I wanted to re-establish the child world, that alliance of mutual loyalty and help through which children get their first experience of equality. Supported and comforted by each other's familiar presence, children can free themselves for a while from total dependence on the monstrous regiment of grown-ups.

I had loved watching Sarah and Daniel learn to play and laugh alone together, and develop new roles towards each other. Sarah was often the superior – maternal, bossy, patronising or solicitous – but when Daniel branched out from his allotted part of eager disciple to become a buffoon and joker, Sarah in turn rewarded him with enthusiastic admiration. They invented games and slogans to tease and defy their parents. When we went out to dinner leaving them in *the charge of their nurse, they held each other's hands as they waved goodbye. In flinching from a future in which Daniel would remain an only child, I saw him as a vulnerable figure, always in the company of alien giants who could never fully respond to his carefree gaiety.*

Femininity, the child world, and of course a renewal of the delight in watching a new human being grow and flourish, these seemed to be impersonal gifts of parenthood which countless parents have experienced. I thought they would be restored to us if we adopted a baby. So, with a somewhat desperate hope, I started to investigate the possibilities of adoption. Meanwhile the conversations with Daniel about Sarah continued.

December 7

We went to a big party last night, the first, and took Daniel because our hosts had told us they had a flying fox in the garden that he would enjoy riding on. I succeeded in not mentioning Sarah at all. I try not to talk about her because people are embarrassed and have nothing to say, or if they do manage to say anything it is not enough for me and I feel disappointed. Also because I must learn to manage without the sustaining illusion that the marvellous gifts and acts of my children magnify my own stature. At least in regard to her, who no longer exists for others. But I didn't find much else to talk about, and felt bored and uncomfortable. I drank two glasses of champagne.

I left early to take Daniel home, and when we were in the car I couldn't restrain myself any longer from talking about her. I said to Daniel, 'Sarah would have liked that party.' And somehow I found myself describing her 'at the angels''.

'Sarah is laughing, and she says "My Feddy-Puss has been to a party. I wish I could be there with him." Our Sarah is looking down at us and laughing and saying to the angels, "That's my Feddy down there."' We both enjoyed sharing this fantasy.

On the way home Daniel asked, 'Why did Sarah die? Is Matthew going to die? Are Viva and Tammy going to die?' And he asked me all the way home whether various children were going to die.

This was the only occasion on which I ever spoke as though I could see what was going on at the angels' or know anything about Sarah's present existence there. It was in part due to the champagne, in part to a talk a few days ago with Barbara Falk, when I had voiced my misgivings about the whole angels story. She thought I was being too severe with myself. 'After all, it's very vague.'

I have thought of this scene under the trees of a suburban street on a warm summer night very often, and still do, always with pleasure. Like Daniel, I occasionally played a private game of pretence that Sarah had returned, but this was the only time I shared the pretence with anyone else, and the only time it was accompanied by a feeling that was almost like absolute conviction. Incredulity at the death which one mourns is perhaps the most constant feature of grief. It springs up again and again, thousands of times. But the disbelief is never total. The icy truth had lodged in me the moment I heard the doctor tell me she was dead, and it did not budge, whatever other antics of mind or imagination I performed simultaneously. Except on this one occasion, when for a few minutes it melted away and I seemed to believe that love and longing could really restore her to life.

December 15
Daniel, matter-of-factly: 'I want to die.'
'Well, one of these days you will die.'
'When will I die?'

'I don't know; not for a long time.'
'When I die, will I go to the angels?'
'Yes.'
'And will I see Sarah at the angels'?'
'Yes, you'll see Sarah.'

The dilemma! I don't like what I say but I don't know
what else to do. I suppose my defence is that I have in fact
told him the truth, often, in insisting that Sarah can't
come back and will not come back, ever. And then I have
told him a consoling myth by saying she is with the angels.
And it *has* consoled him; more than that, it seemed to be
unavoidable; it came about almost by itself; I didn't think
about it beforehand and it certainly doesn't represent any
belief of mine. And as Barbara comfortingly said, it is very
vague. But then he asks all these further questions,
pushing for details. Yet I tell myself reassuringly that at
least I haven't fallen into the same trap as Rosa Katz and
Jenny Marston. [*Both these women, one a psychologist whose
conversations with her own children have been published, the other a
personal friend, had felt compelled to allay the bitter distress of a
child afraid of death by assuring him that he need never die.*] I feel
sympathetic towards them, but censorious. The inevita-
bility of death is what children can't in the end avoid
learning and the big inexcusable lie is to deny that fact.

December 26
Daniel: 'Can Sarah talk at the angels'?'
    I don't remember what I said. Probably, 'Yes I think
so.'
    'What are the angels?'
    'Nobody knows much about the angels because only the
people who die see them. They are people with big wings.'
(Not at all happy with my part in this conversation.)

December 27
Daniel: 'Has Sarah got a brain?'
'Yes of course Sarah had a brain. Everybody has a brain. She couldn't have lived without a brain.'
'No, I mean has she got a brain now?'
'No, Sarah hasn't got a body now. Only her spirit is alive now.' (I'm not sure of my exact words – something like this.)
And again questions that are asked very often, almost every day.
Daniel: 'Why did Sarah get very ill?'
'I don't know darling, she just did. No one knows why.'
'How did the germs get in Sarah?'

Daniel: 'Why don't boys die?'
'They sometimes do. Sometimes little girls die, and sometimes little boys die, but not very often. Usually girls and boys grow up to be very old people.'

December 28
Daniel to Erwin, walking from his studio to the kitchen and slipping his hand into Erwin's: 'Feel what a nice warm furry paw I've got. My claws are out.'
Again to Erwin, while they were gathering mulberries: 'Once I saw an eagle sitting on the tree.'
Erwin to me: 'I like that sort of remark.'

December 29
Yesterday he asked, 'Why did you say Sarah was laughing with the angels?'
I saw an occasion to make a bridge between the image of Sarah really somewhere with the angels, and Sarah living only in our thoughts.

I said, 'Because I like to think of Sarah laughing. She had such a lovely laugh, and she laughed so often. She laughed with you and with all of us, and I often remember her beautiful laughing face.'

This morning he returned again to the questions that have been preoccupying him lately, about where Sarah is now and what she is like, did the angels make her lungs better, did they make her heart beat again. I moved a little further than I have done before.

I said something like: 'No, the angels didn't make Sarah's heart beat again. Her heart is part of her body, and when you die your spirit leaves your body. Sarah's spirit is what made her laugh and talk and move and love us, and when she died that went away from her.'

And I told him a bit more about the occasion of her death.

'I wasn't with Sarah when she died. The doctors asked me to wait while they gave her some medicine to make her better. Sarah was still alive then. She was very sick, but she could still move and smile and talk a little, although she was very tired. I waited in a little room for the doctors to come back. Then they came back and they looked very sad, and they told me that Sarah had died. I rang up Daddy and he came to the hospital and then we both went to see Sarah. She was lying on the bed and she looked just like our own beautiful Sarah, but she couldn't move or talk or laugh any more because her spirit had left her body.

'That's the difference between life and death. It's the hardest thing in the world for even grown-ups to understand. And people don't quite know what happens to the spirit – or some people call it the soul – when it leaves the body. It goes to join the spirits of other people who have died. Some of them were very great and wonderful people and they are the ones we call the angels.'

63

Daniel: 'I know, the spirit is your inside.'

'No darling. The things in your inside, your brain and your heart and lungs and stomach, they are all part of your body, and they stay behind when you die.'

Daniel listened quietly and rather seriously while I talked, looking at me. All this was not exactly premeditated, and I had certainly not worked it out in detail. I can see that both the philosophy and the theology are pretty dubious in places. But I had been bothered by his constant return during the last few days to what has happened to Sarah's body and to the various organs which he has heard about. He didn't ask me this morning where her body is now, but I think I have begun to convey that the Sarah who is with the angels is not the bodily Sarah with a heart and lungs.

Daniel went on: 'Did Sarah take her bear with her?'

'No, darling.'

'Why didn't she take her bear?'

'Because she had no body to play with her bear. She couldn't carry it or stroke it.'

'Where is Sarah's bear now?'

'In the cupboard in Daddy's room.'

'I want to see Daddy.'

We went to Erwin's studio and I left him there. When he noticed I wasn't in the room he gave a cry and ran out to the back part of the house. Erwin and I went to him and I explained that I had only gone to the lavatory. He returned easily to playing with his toys.

I came upstairs and started to make the beds. After a few minutes he came up. He started to push his penis out of the front of his underpants. I had explained to him when we bought these new underpants about three months ago, the first he had had with a fly front, that the hole was for pushing his penis through when he wee'd and that the new underpants were like Daddy's, but until today he hadn't tried.

He said, 'Look, I've pushed the whole of my penis through the hole. I want to wee.'

On the way to the lavatory I said, 'I don't think you're quite tall enough to stand on the floor and wee in the lavatory yet. We'll have to get you a box to stand on.'

But it turned out that he was tall enough – only just.

He said, very proudly, 'I wee'd without taking my pants off. You didn't think I was big enough, but I am.'

He went downstairs to see Erwin. I came down a few minutes later, and said 'Did he tell you what he did?'

'No. He helped me pick up staples and he put every one in the waste paper basket. He didn't throw a single one on the floor.'

When I told him about Daniel's achievement, Daniel said, 'I did it just like Daddy. Just like you.'

Erwin and Daniel had been about to go and pick mulberries. I came upstairs to write these notes and they went into the garden together. Then Daniel came upstairs and told me happily, 'I gathered mulberries for tomorrow, for when Noni comes.'

Just as he did when Sarah first died, he responds to being treated in an adult way by another piece of grown-up behaviour, as if to say, 'You have treated me like a grown-up and I will show you that you are right and that I appreciate it, by behaving like a grown-up.' But none of this is over-solemn or beyond his years. He looks happy and is now in the bath, playing as usual.

1965

January 5

Not until a few weeks ago, when I read a chapter called 'A Death in the Family' in Dr Spock's *Problems of Parents*, did it occur to me that Daniel might feel guilt over Sarah's death. Spock suggests that the death of a parent or sibling will stir up in a young child the guilt he felt on past occasions when he hurt, or wanted to hurt, the dead person, leading him to believe that his own evil wishes caused the death. Last night I read Sylvia Anthony's *The Child's Discovery of Death*, which includes a discussion of the same theme.

I can't recall any signs of guilt in Daniel's behaviour, however convincing such arguments may seem.

He was impressed by seeing a film of Snow White on TV last week, and has said repeatedly, 'I'm killing the wicked queen. I've shot her with my gun. She went off in the ambulance. I shot her with Daddy's gun. Daddy said I could . . . I'm Snow White.' (Am I the wicked queen? I don't recall any other signs of that, either.)

January 10

I trod twice on one of Daniel's tractors with bare feet, and hurt my foot. The second time I got cross and said that if he left it there and I trod on it again, I would throw it away. Daniel was upset and cried, and asked me why I said that. I replied that I was cross because I hurt my foot, but that I wouldn't really throw his tractor away.

Later in the day, he fought vigorously when I was trying to wash and change him, smeared soap on the walls, put his finger on the running tap to make the water squirt, etc., and I again got cross with him.

After he was dressed, I said, 'Are you afraid I'd throw you away because I got cross with you?'

Daniel: 'Yes.'

'I wouldn't do that.'

'Why wouldn't you?'

'Because you're my own beautiful Daniel. Even if I sometimes get cross with you, I love you very much and I wouldn't throw you away.'

Immediately afterwards, Daniel asked, 'Why did Sarah die?'

'Because she got very sick. It wasn't because we got cross with her or didn't love her. We loved her very much and didn't want her to die.'

Daniel asked yet once more about Sarah and the angels, not in his usual serious way but with a rather malicious-looking smile which made me ask, 'Are you cross with Sarah because she died and left you?'

'Yes.'

January 26

I think Daniel talks more than usual about Sarah during this holiday period, just as he did during our Sydney trip. Some of his recent remarks: 'This is my window, and that's Daniel's' (in the car). 'Those are my things. I'm Sarah.' 'Sarah is jumping down the steps.' 'Is that Sarah's windcheater?' (of a windcheater I was about to put on him. He likes to wear clothes that were hers.) 'Those used to be Sarah's,' of a pair of corduroy pants which he hasn't worn for about six months and which Sarah hadn't worn for at least two years.

January 28
Yesterday at Betty's pool, Daniel was swimming around cheerfully and self-confidently as usual, supported by the plastic wings. I heard him say to himself, not uncheerfully, like a reassurance and answer to his longings, 'Sarah's a long long way away, at the angels'.'

February 1
Daniel: 'Do crocodiles die?'
   'Yes.'
   'Why do they?'
   'Everything dies sooner or later.'
   'I don't want to die.'
   'Well I hope you won't die until you're an old old man, older than Grandpa.'
   'I don't want to die even when I'm an old man.'
   'I'll tell you something darling, a lot of people feel the same. I feel the same. But there's just nothing we can do about it.'
   'Will I see Sarah when I die?'
   'I don't know darling.'
   'Why don't you?'
   'Nobody knows much about what happens when you die. Some people think that you'll see Sarah.'
   But this time his span of concentration on the subject was shorter. Already he wasn't really listening to my last reply, and he ran off to look for the kittens.

February 18
Daniel: 'Why does everything have to die some day?'
    'That's just the way the world works.'
    'Why is it the way the world works?'
    'I don't know. It just is.'
He looked serious but didn't seem anxious. I answered
lightly and laughed, making a face to express rueful
helplessness, a joke in which he joined. I had been thinking over Sylvia Anthony's assertion that children need at
some stage to be given a reassurance of their own immor-
tality. When Daniel's questions are not about Sarah they
are nearly always general. He has seldom referred to his
own death. I did feel driven to make up a tale about Sarah
which implies that she is still somewhere, but I haven't so
far felt the need to deny to Daniel that he himself will die.
And I think perhaps joking and light-hearted play may be
a better reassurance than verbal denial.

February 22
More talk about Sarah's death and about the fact that
everything dies. He repeated the complaint that he didn't
want to die even when he was an old man. This time I said
that when he was an old man he might be quite glad to die,
that the next person to die would probably be Aunty Nell,
and that she had told me she would be quite glad to die.
She is old and weak, and can hardly see, and her husband
and both her sisters are dead, so she feels that she is quite
ready.
    This must have impressed him, because he asked me a
bit later, 'Why did Aunty Nell say she would be glad to
die?'
    I felt uncomfortable at breaking the taboo against
talking about the imminent deaths of people we know, but
it is true that she may die soon, and I thought that the idea

that people can be glad to die, although it probably seems very remote, might do something to counterbalance his own fear. Also, the day before I had read Swift's description of the struldbrugs, those miserable degraded beings condemned to grow ever older with no prospect of release – an unanswerable demonstration of the ultimate desirability of death.

But I made another remark about death yesterday that I am less sure about. Daniel had been very obstreperous, alternately kicking, biting and scratching Erwin and me, and then laughing, kissing us, and rolling around on the ground. When I was changing him into his pyjamas, he suddenly threw himself at me and hit my temple quite hard with his forehead. I got cross because it hurt, and because I'd had enough of his rough play.

He said, 'I'll kiss it!' but I replied, 'That won't stop it hurting. Things can't be undone once they are done. We can't bring Sarah back to life, and you can't stop my head hurting now you've hit it. It'll only gradually get better.'

All in all, yesterday he had a strong dose of the stubborn endurance of reality. Perhaps too much – probably that last observation of mine was unnecessary. And yet the harsh facts that I refused to deny to Daniel are not my invention. I have thought over Sylvia Anthony's suggestion that a denial that they themselves will die is a comfort some children need at a certain stage. Rightly or wrongly, I don't feel that I can or should give this comfort to him, and nor does Erwin. The fact of Sarah's death is plain to him, and I think it is gradually also becoming clearer that he will never see her again. He asks less often about the angels. I have recorded how about a fortnight ago when he first talked of his own death and asked would he see Sarah, I said I didn't know. I haven't heard him since then talk of Sarah as being with the angels, or as still existing in any way except when he himself is Sarah, which is still a great deal of the time.

Today he has been clinging and easily moved to tears, which is unusual. He cried because Erwin didn't want his company while he dressed to go into town. Daniel and I waved goodbye, and then I read to Daniel from the poetry book. I read a poem which Sarah used to like, about a cat and the possibility that a fox might catch her while she was out hunting mice for her kittens. Daniel's eyes filled with tears, the first time I have known him react in such a way to a book. So I embroidered on the other half of the poem, the cat returning safely home with food for her kittens' dinner. He slowly cheered up, and then I read 'The Owl and the Pussycat', which he liked and wanted me to repeat.

He is very young to have to face the reality of death, but it is chance which has brought that about. It doesn't seem to me that we would help him by denying what the world has so plainly demonstrated. I have indeed tried denying it, but haven't been able to sustain the denial. Perhaps if I had foreseen more clearly where the denial was to lead – I mean the story about Sarah being up with the angels – we might have prepared ourselves to be more consistent. I don't know whether that would have been better or not. I do feel that those who encouraged us to use the angels story didn't know how often he would return to it, or what a wealth of detail he would demand. Barbara said 'It's very vague,' but it isn't always vague; he wants to know exact details. I always planned to drop the story quietly when he was ready to face the truth. Now I seem to have dropped it earlier than I intended to, because I was not equal to the need for consistency.

After writing these notes, I started on impulse to write to Cecily to ask her advice about the angels story. Then I screwed up the letter. I couldn't possibly explain enough of what has happened for her comments to be worth anything. She could only say – you must do what seems right. So I didn't finish the letter.

During the previous months I had been pursuing the possibilities of finding a baby to adopt. The first enquiries made it apparent that I had two heavy black marks against me, bereavement and age, of which the second seemed to be regarded as the more serious handicap. It was a rule of adoption authorities that no parent should be more than forty years older than her adopted child, and I was already forty-four. But opposition on grounds that seemed to me irrational had only made me more determined, and I worked hard. I talked to friends and acquaintances, read books, was interviewed by hospital matrons and adoption society social workers, visited dubious doctors with seedy practices, appealed to society ladies engaged in good works, and met families with adopted children. The amateurs at least were all in favour of adoption. No one recalled a situation that had turned out badly, and in general this was true of books also. The suggestion that I might not know my own feelings was usually made by social workers and hospital matrons, women who held the power of decision, and I resented their intrusiveness.

Finally I met someone who was both sympathetic and able to help, an eminent old gentleman who had recently remarried after the death of a beloved first wife. He talked composedly about personal tragedy ('It's a funny old thing, life') and about his conviction that it was right to try to rebuild happiness, and he introduced me to Sister Considine, the matron of a small home for unmarried mothers and their babies. I got on well with Sister Considine, and had long talks with her about Sarah and about her own work with mothers and babies. The mothers especially aroused in her a wry tenderness. She visited our house, the only time I ever progressed so far, told me I was a marvellous mother, and described a couple whose as yet unborn child, if a girl, might be suitable for us.

In due course a girl was born and we went to see her. She did not immediately tug at our heartstrings. I would have said 'She is not the one,' had I not been afraid that we would never be given a second chance. We agreed to take her. She could have come home with us then and there, but we decided to wait until she was a month old, when the mother would forfeit her right to change her mind.

March 30

We took Daniel to Lorne for the weekend before we were due to bring the new baby home. He was quiet and subdued much of the time. He had a bit of a cold, but I think it was more than that, I think he was remembering our visits there with Sarah and missing her. We had lunch by an abandoned timber-mill where there was marvellous lumber lying around – rusting trucks, an old cart, and the wooden top from a cattle truck. He played around, but only for a very short while, quietly and nervously. I suggested that the cattle truck made a good emu cage, but he only played at being an emu in it for a few moments. Then he went and sat in the car.

I told him on the Monday afternoon that next day we would be bringing the new little baby sister home. He accepted the news quietly, without excitement, only asking 'Why are you?' in the unfocused way that is typical of the moment. He asks 'Why?' often, and apparently indiscriminately. E.g., I recalled that we had seen a lizard on a log in the country, about so long – and I showed him with my hands.

Daniel: 'Why did we see a lizard so long?'

He repeated the question several times, although I replied that it just *was* 'so long'. I think he is seeking answers to questions too complex for him to formulate – wants to know 'all about it', without knowing quite what to ask.

Next morning I took him with me shopping while I bought feeding bottles and plastic pants for the baby. He wasn't excited, though not as solemn as he had been the day before. I asked him what we should call her. He said 'Sarah', and I explained that we couldn't call her Sarah because she wouldn't be Sarah, she would be a new sister. A few blocks further on, he returned to the familiar question, not asked for several weeks, 'Why did Sarah die?'

It was only when we brought the baby home that he was suddenly transformed with excitement and joy. His face shone when he looked at her, and watched her being fed. He asked to touch her bottle, and then her head. I took him round to Betty's in the afternoon and he announced loudly and proudly, 'We've got a new baby, but I've got to wait until she's bigger until I can play with her.'

That was a week ago, and he has been in cheerful, often boisterous spirits ever since – markedly happier than before the baby came, although most of the time he takes little notice of her. On Sunday I had breakfast in bed and then fed the baby in bed. He came and snuggled in beside me and we talked confidentially about the baby. I feel it is a new interest we have in common. His bent is so decidedly masculine that I have sometimes felt that there isn't much we can share.

Like Sarah's death, the baby's arrival has spurred Daniel to new feats. Almost every night since she came, he has put himself to bed on the playroom couch swiftly and without fuss, pulled the rug over himself, and gone immediately to sleep, instead of demanding our company while he dozed off.

There have been new questions also. A conversation from two days after she arrived:

Daniel: 'If the cat has more kittens, where will they come from?' Erwin had mentioned the possibility.

'They'll grow inside her like the last ones.'

'But how will they get inside her?'

'They grow from something very tiny, called an egg, but very very small. And then it grows bigger and bigger until it turns into a kitten.' (Pause while I reflected that this was fobbing him off a bit.) 'Actually there are two eggs, one from the Daddy, called a seed, and one from the Mummy, and when they come together they start growing and turn into a baby – a human baby if it's a woman and a baby kitten if it's a cat.' (The question of where babies come from had never been asked before.)

Daniel: 'But who is the kittens' daddy?'

'One of those big old toms that come sneaking around to eat the cats' food. There are two of them, a big grey and a ginger one. I don't know which one is the kittens' daddy, but I think it's one of them.'

We named the baby Sylvia. I believe that her arrival was welcomed by members of my family as carrying the possibility of solace and hope. But I did not feel any of the calmly besotted joy that enveloped me when I brought home my own children, nor even the triumphant excitement I had once observed when a previously childless friend had visited us to show off her newly-acquired foster-child. Only a stoical conviction that I was doing what had to be done.

I looked after Sylvia for a whole year and remember her hardly at all. I have no photograph, and wrote very little about her in any of the journals. The few notes I did make remind me that most of the time I managed to sustain a dogged patience in caring for her. I usually had the help of a nurse in the daytime, but at night and at weekends she was in my sole charge. I didn't ask Erwin to share the work as I would have done had she been his child. With or without love, a baby needs a lot of attention, and Sylvia was not a happy baby. She cried a lot and it was difficult to get her to sleep.

At first there doubtless was some solace in the routine of looking after a helpless and dependent being, and I was touched when later she began to greet my appearance with smiles, and when she and Daniel laughed together. But soon I found myself struggling with surges of rage because she wasn't Sarah, repelled by her pale pudgy body, and resenting the endless chores.

Yet during most of the year, whenever I wondered whether we should continue with the attempt to make her a part of our family, I had a renewed vision of the strength and gaiety of the child-world alliance between her and Daniel that seemed to lie just ahead. I reminded myself of the saying of Homer Lane, that one learns to love an alien and unappealing child by acting as though one already loves her. So although I didn't make any move to institute the formalities of legal adoption, some hope still infused the duties of looking after Sylvia. These form a continuous hidden background to the exchanges with Daniel about Sarah's death, which remain the almost exclusive subject of the Diary.

April 8

Daniel still talks a great deal about Sarah – what she did, what she liked, where they went together. He doesn't say 'When Sarah was alive' now, but 'When Sarah was here' – accepting the fact of her disappearance and for the moment by-passing the mysteries. Occasionally, if he has been talking of himself as Sarah, he will say, 'When Sarah was here really . . .' Several times he has said, 'I'm Sarah and the baby is Daniel,' or 'I know, let's call her Daniel.' I never deny it when he says he is Sarah, but I very rarely call him Sarah in return. But I did yesterday and he said 'No, I'm not Sarah. I'm Feddy.' Being Feddy is a frequent game these days and he quite clearly associates the name with her.

He also likes to play at being an eagle or a snake. Last night, after returning from the country, he played at being an eagle in the kitchen, flapping his wings and then folding them on his chest, and putting on a severe eagle-expression, sucking in his lower lip. We had seen an eagle sitting on a tall dead tree on the way to Woods Point on Wednesday. We stopped the car and watched it for a few minutes. Then it flew off, but circled around near us, alternately flapping its wings and gliding.

Erwin asked him, 'Are you the eagle we saw sitting on the tree in the mountains?'

'No, I'm not that eagle, because I'm bigger than that eagle. I'm a very big eagle, but I'm not as big as you.'

April 22

Daniel went to the museum today with Margaret [*his new nurse, an intelligent and very attractive girl, much the nicest of all the nurses we had after Sarah died*]. I have promised to take him and several times he has refused to go with Margaret, but perhaps he is losing hope that I will, because three days ago he asked if he could go with Margaret, and eagerly repeated the question each morning.

He reported on his return, 'I saw snakes at the museum. The snakes were dead but they said Hullo to me. Why are the snakes at the museum dead?' (I attempted an explanation in terms of it being easier to keep them if they were dead, but he didn't listen.) 'The snakes were in a glass case. I saw a wedge-tailed eagle. The eagles didn't have a glass case around them. The eagle wanted to fly home with me. The eagle is my sister.'

May 4
It is hard to imagine what she must have been for him. Not a limited figure enclosed by boundaries of time and space and personality, standing out against the background of all that was not her. More like the sun and the earth, part of the essential nature of the universe. He had always known her and never spent a night apart from her in all his life. Then suddenly she disappeared, totally, without warning.

May 5
Daniel: 'Tell me about when I was a baby and Sarah was a little girl.'

'Well we came out from England to Australia in an aeroplane, and you had a little cot which hung on the wall, because you were like the baby, you couldn't sit up, you could only lie down. And you had your own safety belt to fasten you into the cot. When the plane takes off they call out "Fasten your seat belts," and Mum had to fasten her own seat belt and Daniel's too.'

Daniel: 'Not Daniel, Feddy.'

'No, that was before you were called Feddy. Feddy was Sarah's name for you, but she hadn't started to call you Feddy then.'

'What did Sarah have that she died of?'

'She had flu very badly.'

'Would she have died if she'd had a bad cough?' (Not asked with any obvious anxiety, but he has had a cough recently.)

'I don't think so. I've never heard of anyone dying of a cough.'

'But if she'd had a cough as bad as she had the flu?'

'I still don't think she would have died. You see the germs were in her lungs, where the air goes when you

79

breathe, and the germs made her lungs full of mucus. You know when you have a cold there's mucus in your nose. Well Sarah's lungs were filled with mucus that the germs made. And then once when she tried to breathe, a big lump of mucus blocked her throat and she couldn't breathe. That's how she died. If you can't breathe you die.'

During this conversation I had been washing and changing the baby, and then putting her to bed. When I had finished, I took Daniel on my knee and started my usual consolation-piece about how no one knew she was going to die and no one wanted her to die. The discussion ended as many have – he slipped off my knee, looking still a bit solemn, but not as if deliberately closing the discussion – absent-mindedly, as if his interest in the subject were for the moment satisfied and his attention turned to something else.

Later in the morning. Daniel is swinging alone and quietly on the swing, the first time I have seen him there for weeks – handsome Daniel, who talked this morning of Sarah's death so rationally. He longs for her and doesn't understand why she disappeared. I can't picture his memories of her, but his longing must be as great as ours and the place she held in his life as totally unfillable. So young to know such a grief, such a disappearance, a parting that is unwanted and for ever. He has great courage and gaiety, which alternates with solemnity. Margaret has come to call him to lunch; he started laughing as he showed off some trick to her, and now he runs in to lunch with her as he used to run with Sarah, chasing each other round the path.

May 6
We talked about the possibility of making a trip to Queensland, and I told Daniel that we would stop in a different motel every night.

Daniel: 'Can't we leave today?'

'No, because we would have to pack our clothes and arrange for someone to look after Grandma and Grandpa.'

Daniel: 'Grandma can come with us.'

'No I don't think she can because we'll have the baby, so there wouldn't be room for Grandma.'

'But why must we take the baby?'

'Well, she's our baby now, we couldn't leave her behind.'

May 9
Another long conversation about Sarah in hospital, and about the angels. It included some new questions.

Daniel: 'How did she get from the hospital to the angels?'

'The people who think she has gone to the angels don't think her body went, only her spirit . . .'

'How did the germs get into Sarah that made her sick?'

'I don't know, I don't think anyone knows. There are plenty of germs around everywhere, but why they made Sarah sick when they didn't make me or Daddy sick, or Alastair or Jamie, I don't know.'

'Would an expert know that?'

'He'd know more about it than we do, but there are lots of things that even an expert doesn't know . . .'

'I want to see a dead elephant.'

'Well you can't do that. There aren't any dead elephants here.'

'Why not?'

'Elephants don't live in this country. There are only the elephants in the zoo and they don't die very often. Elephants live a long time. And even if one of them died, I don't think you would be allowed to see its body.'

'Why not?'

'Because they wouldn't leave it in the enclosure where the live animals are. Its body would start to decay.'

'What would they do with its body?'

'They'd probably bury it.'

'Why?'

'Well that's one of the things people often do with dead bodies.'

It wasn't pursued further. These conversations, which have recurred ever since Sarah died but have been particularly frequent in the past few days, skirting death from many angles, have been more numerous and more rambling and repetitive than I have been able to record. I try to answer, truthfully and calmly but not discursively, whatever Daniel asks. I rather dread his questions about where Sarah's body is now, feeling that it is too soon for him to be told and for me to have to tell, that her body was burned and that her ashes are in a tin box in a suitcase of clothes upstairs. We came near to the question today, but he still did not ask directly, 'Where is Sarah's body now?' or 'Was Sarah buried?'

Yesterday Daniel played at planning to build 'puss-houses' with Alastair and Jamie. After they had gone:

'I'm going to build a puss-house for all the pusses. For the Feddy-puss and the Sylvia-puss and the Mummy-puss and the Daddy-puss and the Mama-puss and the Grandpa-puss.'

'And the Sarah-puss too?' I asked.

'No, because the Sarah-puss isn't alive.'

Why did I ask that? Because I am feeling Sarah's death with particular acuteness in these days after her birthday, the anniversary of the richest and most beautiful weeks of her life. But Daniel seems to make clear that he is the only one to whom fantasy is permitted.

He asked rather plaintively, a little later: 'But why did you say there would be a puss-house for Sarah?'

'I don't know darling. I suppose I thought that they are all pretend puss-houses, so you might like it if we pretended that Sarah was with us in one of them.'

May 10

Yesterday afternoon we went to Fisherman's Bend [*a derelict and desolate reach of the Bay, near the city but too flat and marshy to have been developed*]. Daniel and I walked along a stretch of white beach near the Tasmanian Ferry Terminal. We saw a dead sea bird – a cormorant, I said. Daniel looked at it with interest and asked why it had died. I said perhaps it had been sick, or it might have been shot.

'I want to see another dead cormorant.'

We saw four, and after each Daniel looked ahead eagerly for the next. The birds were not very recently dead; they were spread out very flatly and partly covered with sand. The last one either had no head, or its head was covered with sand. Daniel wanted to see its head, but I said that something, perhaps a dog, had eaten its head off. By then we had come to the end of the beach, and started to walk along a causeway between the sea and a stretch of muddy water.

Daniel said several times, 'I want to see another dead bird with its head on,' but there were no more dead birds. Then at intervals, 'I want to see a dead jackdaw . . . I want to see a dead emu . . . I want to see a dead ostrich.' Then suddenly he returned to a talk we had had in the morning.

'Why isn't Sarah still in hospital?'

'Because Sarah died. What we saw in the hospital was only her body. The real Sarah had died and her body wasn't Sarah at all, so there was no reason to keep it in the hospital.'

When I told Erwin about our conversation on the causeway, he commented, 'He is very different from Sarah. He is like someone who has been to the war compared to someone who stayed home.'

May 11

Daniel and the 'flight to reality'. How calm and unexcited he looks when he asks these questions and listens to our replies; curious but not particularly worried. He often turns straight to a joke afterwards. From did we see Sarah's eyes when we went to the hospital after she died, to did we see her nose etc.

May 28

Daniel has talked less of Sarah lately, and doesn't insist at all that he *is* Sarah, though he is consistently emphatic that he is Feddy, not Daniel. He still asks about her sometimes. When Betty took him to the zoo last week he asked on returning, 'When Sarah was alive, did we go to the zoo and did we see some snakes in a cage with wire?'

He is fascinated by snakes at present, collects whole boxes of them made of sticks, string, shoelaces and plasticine, and asks repeatedly to be allowed to sleep downstairs all night, where 'the snakes will keep me company'.

84

June 1
He went to nursery school for the first time today. He didn't want to go, said he would be lonely, and insisted that I must stay with him all the time, not only today but every day. He played alone most of the time, making snakes out of clay and asking me to help him. Several times he burst into tears when the clay wouldn't do what he wanted, or when I joined broken pieces by 'crossing them over' – not, apparently, the right way. But then he was led outside by the assistant teacher, who had a bubble ring, and stayed out for about twenty minutes, playing in the sandpit. I think it is a not unpromising beginning.

June 3
What seems fairly obviously to be a memory: the adults were talking about spiders.

Daniel: 'One day Sarah showed me a tarantula on the ceiling of the upstairs bathroom.'

June 26
Starting off for school with Daniel. He still protests every morning that he doesn't want to go, and even cries a bit at the prospect, though when it is time to leave he doesn't hang back. I am sure he enjoys it and would be disappointed if I said, 'Well you needn't go', but he likes to protest, as an expression of the part of him that doesn't like being left.

'Can I take Messo [*the cat*] to school?'
'No, they won't let you take cats and dogs to school.'
'Why not?'
'They've got enough to do looking after the children, and the cats might run away. Or they might knock things over, or tear the cushions.'

Daniel, laughing gleefully and enjoying this: 'What else might they do?'

'They might get in the way when you were having music, or put their paws in the clay, or knock things off the nature table, or sniff the milk, or bite someone.' I had to continue this catalogue of misdemeanours all the way to school, egged on by Daniel asking 'What else might they do?', making a few suggestions of his own, and pealing with laughter, of course most loudly at the suggestion that they might wee or poo in the corner. This vision of the undisciplined iconoclastic cat is clearly a welcome release for that side of Daniel which resents the programmed order he is now having to conform to, however gently it is administered.

June 28

Daniel: 'Why isn't Sarah still in the hospital?'

'Because Sarah died, darling.'

'But why isn't she in the hospital?'

'Because when you die there is only your body left and that isn't any good, so it wouldn't be any use them keeping it in the hospital.'

'Did the angels make Sarah better?'

'I don't know darling. No one knows much about what happens when you die because no one has ever come back after they have died. Some people think that you go to the angels and they make you better; and some people think that when you die your life is finished and you don't exist any more.'

Daniel changed the subject. He didn't, has never yet, asked where Sarah's body went, nor which of the two beliefs I hold. He seldom mentions the angels these days, and my answers don't provide the same encouragement that they did at first.

Yesterday Erwin had a slight temperature in the morning and didn't feel well. I told Daniel, and said he could come in and see Erwin but shouldn't make a noise. He tiptoed in very meekly and quietly. Then I sat with him in the playroom having breakfast and feeding the baby. Daniel made snakes, and repeatedly got very cross when the clay did not behave as he wanted it to.

I said, 'Daddy will be all right later. He feels a bit sick, but he's not very sick.'

'I'm not worried about Daddy, I'm worried about the snakes.'

Later in the day, sitting at the kitchen table, he rolled his eyes downwards with a little smirk on his face, as he often used to do to amuse Sarah ('I always make Sarah laugh'), but as I don't remember him doing since she died. He seems in very good spirits lately. During the afternoon, while we were working in the garden, he explained every-thing we were doing to Sylvia, who was sitting in the pram watching. After supper, still in the kitchen, Sylvia was being joggled on my knee and laughing. I asked Daniel if he would like to get on the other knee and he did, saying cheerfully, 'Now you've got two pusses.' But Sylvia didn't like it, looked balefully at Daniel and started to cry. He quietly climbed down, without saying anything.

Later, in his pyjamas, looking sad and tired, he came into the sitting room where I was sitting by the fire, sat beside me and laid his head on my knee.

I asked him, 'What are you thinking about?'

'I'm not thinking about anything.'

'What are you looking at?'

'I don't know.'

I thought he was probably thinking about Sarah, but, remembering his denial in the morning, I didn't say anything. We walk a tightrope. We must be ready to talk, to help him to talk and to understand and accept the terrible truths of life. But he mustn't be made to feel that we are constantly watching his soul.

Several times lately he has said, gazing into my face, 'My tumpkin hurts', when I don't think it does at all, but he has discovered that both Erwin and I become anxious and concerned when he says this. I won't again.

June 29
I collected Daniel and Alastair from nursery school. Daniel was very cheerful. We went to the library, where Daniel selected another snake book; then I looked for books for myself.

Daniel told Alastair, cheerfully and matter-of-factly, 'I've got the snake book at home that used to be Sarah's. Sarah doesn't live at my house any more because she died.' This is the first time I have heard him talk of her death so plainly to a third person.

Alastair, also very matter-of-factly: 'When are you going to die, Daniel?' Alastair is almost exactly the same age as Daniel, but he hasn't been forced to learn the reality of death. Daniel didn't appear to take in the question, although Alastair repeated it.

Daniel: 'My name isn't Daniel, it's Feddy. A long time ago when I was a tiny baby I was called Daniel, but now I'm called Feddy.'

Although he talks calmly about Sarah's death, Daniel doesn't want to recognise other deaths in his world. About four weeks ago, two of the cats were ill. The favourite didn't eat anything for three days but then recovered. The other male was reported by Margaret to be lying dead in

88

the garden, outside the laundry. She said that Daniel had seen it, so when the moment seemed appropriate I said something to him about the cat having died. Daniel objected forcefully, almost in tears, 'It isn't dead. It's asleep.'

I didn't press the point, and Erwin removed the body without saying anything to him. Daniel has never asked where the cat was, and we haven't talked about it as we do about Sarah. I feel that one death is enough for him to cope with.

Two days ago he found a furry caterpillar in the garden, curled up in a ball, and put it in a tin. We talked about what sort of leaves it might like to eat.

Because I hadn't seen it move, I suggested that it might be dead.

Daniel, again very forcefully: 'It isn't dead, it's alive.'

Perhaps he had seen it move – it certainly was alive in the evening, and we watched it together, 'galloping' around the tin.

One of Daniel's most desolate experiences after Sarah died was sleeping alone in the room they had shared, where they had played rough sexy games on her bed, listened to stories together and then 'read' companionably before the light was put out, and woken together in the morning. His first attempt to change this had been to move into her bed, some weeks after she died. Later, he took to falling asleep downstairs, on the playroom couch, and being carried up to his own room when we went to bed. Sometimes he would just fall asleep on the sitting-room floor. On the rare occasions when we went out to dinner we took him with us, in pyjamas and dressing-gown. He would play around on the floor while we ate, and then unobtrusively fall asleep under the table. Then he started objecting to being taken to his upstairs bedroom at all, and demanding to be allowed to sleep all night downstairs.

The loneliness of that bedroom has been an abiding impression. Twenty years later, returning from a mountain trek in Nepal, he commented on how lucky the Nepalese peasant children were to sleep in a warm smelly huddle with their parents and siblings and a dog or two.

July 10

Daniel, last night before going to sleep on the couch: 'I don't like sleeping in my room. I don't like sleeping by myself.'

This complaint has been made every week or so now for months, and he has asked to be allowed to stay downstairs. When I have said that he would be more lonely there, because we would not be close by to come to him if he called in the night, he has said, 'The snakes will keep me company.' I think this is both a longing for Sarah and a desire to sleep in our room. Since I couldn't console him with either of these, I said, 'When Sylvia is a bit older, she can sleep in your room if you like.'

'But I mightn't like her. I don't know what she will be like. What will her face look like?'

'I don't know. People's faces change as they get older. You'll look different in three or four years, and no one knows what you will look like then.' I said this because I didn't want him to think that it is because Sylvia is adopted that we don't know what she will look like. His reference to changing faces is an odd coincidence, because I had been reflecting on how much Sarah had changed in her lifetime, having found some photographs taken when she was two in which I scarcely recognised her.

Also yesterday, he asked, 'How small are germs? Are they as small as Sylvia?'

'No, they are much smaller than Sylvia.'

'Why are they?'

'Because they're so small you can't see them.'

'Are they as small as air?'

A few days ago he asked, 'Is glass air that's close together?'

July 12

I opened a tin of tunny-fish for Daniel's lunch. He looked pleased, and chanted 'Fish, fish, my favourite dish!' Then, 'Did Sarah say "Fish, fish, my favourite dish"?'

'Yes she did.'

'Why did she?'

'Because she liked fish and that was a way of showing she was pleased we were going to have it. Are you thinking about Sarah? I've been thinking about her a lot too lately, and missing her.'

'But you don't need to worry about Sarah . . .' He paused long enough for me to speculate that he might be going to say 'because the angels have made her better', but what he did say was 'because you've got me.'

July 15

Daniel has repeatedly asked me lately what germs look like. 'Do germs look like that?', holding his fingers in a circle.

'I don't know much about what germs look like, but there are different kinds. Some look like little sticks and some like strings of sausages. I can buy you a book about them if you like.'

'I'd rather have a book about scorpions.' We have been searching unsuccessfully in his books for pictures of scorpions.

Yesterday in the kitchen Daniel asked, 'Is choking the same as coughing?' I talked about mucus as one cause of coughing, and how Sarah choked because she couldn't cough away the mucus that was blocking her throat. He asked further questions: Why didn't the doctors make Sarah better? Why did Sarah's spirit go up in the air when she died? Did the angels make her better? Then he talked about the games of chasey they used to play. Did she lift up her feet high when she ran? He started to play chasey by himself, with the old gleeful laugh, but it didn't last long.

I have occasionally talked about some trait of Sarah's, or about something that happened during her life, without Daniel having first mentioned her. But I have never since the first weeks talked about her illness, or death, or what happened after she died, except when he has asked.

July 20
A cold Sunday afternoon, alone at home with the children. Daniel was rather bored so I started to read to him from *A Puffin Book of Verse*. I read three or four poems with moderate success. Then I chose 'The Babes in the Wood', not because of its theme but because the lines were short.

> My dear, do you know
> How a long time ago,
> Two poor little children,
> Whose names I don't know,
> Were stolen away,
> On a fine summer's day,
> And left in a wood,
> As I've heard people say.

And when it was night,
So sad was their plight,
The sun it went down,
And the moon gave no light!
They sobbed and they sighed,
And they bitterly cried,
And the poor little things,
They lay down and died.

And when they were dead,
The robins so red
Brought strawberry leaves
And over them spread;
And all the day long,
They sang them this song –
Poor babes in the wood!
Poor babes in the wood!
And won't you remember
The babes in the wood?

It was a huge success and I had to read it at least ten times, while Daniel grinned with pleasure, and asked questions. Why did they die? Why were they stolen away? Why didn't the robins feed them on strawberries? I suppose there was some trace of anxiety, but there is no doubt of Daniel's pleasure in hearing this little poem. It was probably of the same kind as I get from poems and stories and talk about death – a mixed relief whose two most important elements are the demonstration that one is not alone and hasn't suffered a unique and unprecedented blow, but something that has happened to others; and the objectification of grief, which, once it is embodied in a poem, can be contemplated as something outside oneself.

I remember thinking a long while ago, almost a year ago, that since Daniel resembled us in his reaction in so many ways, he would probably also like to hear stories of death, but I hadn't put this intuition into practice, and had forgotten it.

July 21

In the car on the way to school Daniel said, 'I'm going to have a zoo and an aquarium. And I'm going to have alligators and snakes and monkeys and lions in the zoo. And I'll show you all my animals. The lions will be walking up and down their cage when I take you to see them.'

'I suppose they'll be hungry.'

'Yes, and Daddy will give me some meat for them. They'll have a huge hunk of roast pork. And my aquarium will be open at the top.'

'Oh, why is that?'

'So that the octopuses can get out and go for a walk on the grass.'

July 28

It is not only when it's time for bed that Daniel complains of the loneliness of his room. Lately he has sometimes woken in the night, or when I have carried him upstairs, and cried in a terrible way. The only way I have found to help him then is to involve him in some pleasant fantasy, of his being a zoo-keeper with many animals, or a strong carpenter as big as Daddy. He will start to listen, stop crying, and soon fall asleep again, whereas questions about his comfort or needs are only met by continuous crying.

Last night when I went to carry him up to bed, the little ginger cat was lying on the couch beside his head, and when I came into the room she put a paw on his shoulder.

I carried him safely up to bed but later he awoke crying.

'Do you know what I saw when I came to carry you up to bed tonight?' I asked.

Daniel, through his sobbing and tears, 'What?'

I told him about the cat. He didn't say anything but his crying stopped immediately, and after a few minutes he was asleep.

August 1

At lunch, Daniel was kicking the underside of the table. Erwin first told him to stop, and then held his feet firmly with his own legs. Daniel retaliated by tipping the chair backwards; Erwin told him not to, but Daniel continued. Erwin said, 'You're not to do that, and I mean it very seriously. The chair might tip over backwards and you might fall and cut your head badly and have to go to hospital. Stop it!'

Daniel looked very upset and fought to hold back his tears. It was at one and the same time a defeat by his father, a weighty reprimand, and a threat of death. He stopped tilting the chair, but also found a way to neutralise these disagreeable attacks on his ego.

'I won't fall. An eagle will swoop down and catch me with his wings.'

'Or a pussycat,' Erwin suggested.

'No, an eagle.'

August 4

Daniel: 'Who said, "Sit on me"? Did Sarah say "Sit on me"?' Yes, she did.

August 5

Erwin left for Sydney last night. We have been discussing the trip for weeks without attempting to hide it from Daniel but, probably because he is less demonstrative than Sarah, it hadn't occurred to either of us to talk to him directly about it. But during the afternoon we each noticed that he was perturbed. Erwin went out in the car during the afternoon; Daniel saw him go and said to Margaret that Daddy had gone to Sydney. When Margaret reported this to Erwin on his return, he was very upset to think that Daniel could believe he would go off without a word of goodbye. With me, he displayed the kind of negativism he hasn't shown for a long time. I praised what he had been building with his blocks:

'That's a lovely battleship.'

Daniel: 'It isn't a battleship.'

'What is it?'

'It isn't anything.' He spoke in the same cross flat tone of voice he used after Sarah died.

After observing these incidents, we talked to him about where Erwin was going, where he would stay, why he was going, and when he would be back. Daniel brightened up. I thought that if we had told him a year ago that Sarah had gone for a holiday and would return soon, as some friends advised us, he wouldn't believe us now. As it is, he is not entirely convinced. He has scarcely mentioned Erwin since he left. But his doubt can't be as deep as it would have been, with good reason, had we lied about Sarah.

August 8

I was discussing with Daniel his coming birthday, when he will be four.

Daniel: 'I'm as old as Sarah now.'

'Not quite. Sarah was five when she died. She would have been six now.'

'Do you go on growing after you're dead?' he asked.

'I don't know.'

Why didn't I say simply 'No'? Because I've become very uncertain about how to deal with these questions. But I don't think it matters that much – I think this is an age of uncertainty, of optimism mingled with a slowly growing realisation of the truth – probably of different stages of understanding oscillating with each other. I wouldn't want to give in entirely to encouraging an optimistic picture of Sarah living just around the corner, the same as ever. It involves one in too many contradictions, too great a strain to be consistent, awkward questions from Daniel and the danger of not being believed – because evidence of death appears often and unexpectedly, like those dead seabirds at the beach. Danger also of losing credibility, so that one's explanations of less terrible situations, such as Erwin's visit to Sydney, wouldn't be believed.

I think we didn't do too badly over Erwin's visit to Sydney, but clearly Daniel still has some anxiety. He was more than usually aggressive yesterday. In the morning he suddenly picked up the cat and dropped it into the playpen where the baby was lying, on top of her, so that she was scratched; and at lunchtime he suddenly pinched Mama very hard – both unprecedented things. This morning as soon as he got up he asked eagerly, 'Where's Daddy?' although I had told him last night that Daddy won't be back until very late today.

There is a recurring optimism in his questions about Sarah (some of them), that unquenchable optimism of childhood that Kornei Chukovsky describes so enthusias-

97

tically. I particularly like Chukovsky's story about an eight-year-old's comment on a film: 'Ania, I went to see *Chapayev* ten times and still he was drowned at the end. Maybe if I go with my dad . . .?' – although I suspect it of being apocryphal. But it's not obvious what practical moral one draws from this recurrent optimism. It doesn't follow that death should always be denied. Probably it varies from child to child, but I should think that in general one shouldn't leave death out but needn't strain too hard for consistency. The lines between fantasy and truth are not so sharply drawn in childhood. A truth so basic and enormous as that of death, and the death of one's loved sister, is not accepted the first time it is heard, but by coming back and back to it. You don't need to tell the full horror each time. And I haven't of Sarah.

August 11

Watching from my balcony Daniel playing in the garden. In a sense he has by now recovered from Sarah's death. He plays cheerfully and self-containedly, has plenty to occupy himself with, seldom looks stricken, and is usually absorbed in what he is doing, and often cheerful; he rarely wakes in the night. Of course he will never be the same as he was before. He often talks of her, and asks about her life and her death.

Games played recently:
  making snakes with play dough
  trying to attach the new trapeze to a tree
  building with blocks
  playing with picture blocks
  looking at pictures in library books and his own books
  playing fishing with hook, rope and chain

playing road-mending on the path, with sand and
   Dinky toys
playing at planting plants on the path
swinging
hammering and sawing
pretending that tree branches and leaves are fish and
   sharks

August 14
Sarah's accurate use of long and unusual words, and her
often complex sentence structure, used to delight us, but
now we remember only a general impression; hardly a
single thing she said remains. But now Daniel begins to
say things which remind me of her, and he is still a year
younger than she was when she died. E.g., today, 'I
smelled something in the lock-up cupboard but I didn't
know what it was. And then I found out – chocolate
biscuits!' (dramatically, with exaggerated surprise). Or
yesterday, on returning from the Botanical Gardens. 'We
couldn't see the swans. We walked and walked, and then,
finally – swans!'

August 17
The usefulness of animals in the lives of children. Daniel's
chief pleasure for weeks after Sarah died was feeding the
ducks and swans. They are real and alive, their respon-
siveness makes them more satisfying than stories. They
are uncomplicated – they come, eat, and go away, and
little else. Their status is ambiguous. They allow one to be
the superior, the parent who gives food, and they are often
small in size, but they are also strong and independent.
   The swans were Sarah – he used to talk about the
Sarah-swan. Yet they are not too close to the painful

reality; they do not constantly remind one that they are *not* beautiful lost Sarah.

August 18
Daniel produced what certainly appears to be a memory, although I don't recollect the occasion.

'Once when Sarah and I were away, we leaned over a bridge and saw a lot of fishes swimming around, but Mummy said they weren't fishes, they were tadpoles.'

August 26
I took Daniel, three days before his fourth birthday, to see Aunt Nell. He had taken along one of his snake books and showed her the pictures in it.

'That's the tail of a rattle snake, and that's what it would look like if you cut it through the middle.'

Leaning across to show her, he put his hand on her cigarette, and jumped back.

Aunt Nell: 'I'm very sorry darling. Does it hurt?'

Daniel, standing very straight, the corners of his lips quivering: 'It doesn't hurt, it doesn't hurt at all.' Then it became too much for him and he rushed to me and cried tempestuously from hurt and fright.

I told him afterwards that he was very brave not to cry.

Daniel: 'But I did cry.'

'Yes so you did, but not at first, and that was very brave.'

I don't recall either Erwin or I telling him that a brave boy doesn't cry when he is hurt. Certainly there has been nothing like a continuous effort to instil this sort of bravery. I want to attribute it to a natural sense of dignity, and I am sure that is part of it. But I remember that he was present when Erwin burned his arm on the scalding oily water spurting from the car radiator, and he probably noticed and perhaps thought about the fact that Erwin didn't cry – though I don't recall his commenting or asking about it at the time.

August 30
Daniel asked me if he could have another balloon like one I had bought him a few weeks ago.

'I'll buy you one next time I go to Myers.'

Daniel, doubtfully, 'But we got that one in town.'

'Yes, at Myers when we went to town together.'

'Are there two Myers?'

'Yes, there's Myers in town and Myers at Chadstone.'

Daniel, very relieved: 'I went there with Gunn [*one of his nurses*]. She bought me a plastic saw. There weren't any metal ones so she bought me a plastic one.' This must have been before Christmas, as Gunn left just after Christmas.

September 1
'When was I Daniel and not Feddy when Sarah was here?'

'It was Sarah who first called you Feddy. She made up the name. She used to say, "This is Feddy my puss-cat. He's a nice little cat, he doesn't scratch or bite." And you would make your puss-face. Do you remember?'

Daniel, listening with a happy smile: 'Yes.'

I added, 'And if people said "Freddy?" she would say, "No, Feddy!" And you'll always be Sarah's Feddy-puss.'

'How can I be Sarah's Feddy when she isn't here any more?'

Of course he is right in a way. I tried to say something about always keeping the memory of Sarah's love. I am sure that is what he is doing when he insists, as he always

does, that his name is Feddy, though I don't think that my
abstract explanation got across.

September 3
Daniel: 'It's only a joke when I say I don't like Sylvia.'
   Last week he said to my cousin Jim whom he had never
met before, 'I don't like Sylvia.'
   Jim: 'Oh, why not?'
   Daniel: 'She smells!' Embarrassed silence. He has
sometimes given me the same reason for saying he doesn't
like her.
   But in the last week or so he has enjoyed amusing her
and making her laugh. E.g., he leans over her and chants,
in a monotone except for a rising inflection on the last
syllable, 'Did you see Fed doing a paint – ing?'
   In the garden, wanting to put the baby's pram where I
could watch him, I asked, 'Where are you going to play,
Fed?'
   Daniel, scornfully, over his shoulder: 'I *work*.'
   When I reported this to Margaret she said, 'Yes, he
won't let me say "play" at all. He won't let me call it the
playroom, it has to be the workroom.'

September 8
Gina came to play yesterday morning. Of all the nursery
school children, she reminds me most of Sarah, because of
her lively face and her trusting approach to people (i.e. to
me). She and Daniel played nicely for an hour or so.
Daniel showed her his tools and his fishing line, and Gina
played with Sarah's dolls' pram and dolls. Then Daniel
started to get grizzly and petulant. I thought perhaps he
might be getting measles after all (yesterday had been
the end of the incubation period after a contact). But in

the afternoon, after Gina had gone, he seemed cheerful and energetic enough, and played in the garden with Margaret and Mama. Clearly not getting measles! But not entirely happy. Twice in the day he attacked Sylvia and made her yell, hitting her in the face, and then blowing at her with the balloon pump.

It was a day when I was suffering more acutely than usual from grief for Sarah, because I had been writing about her birth and had suddenly been devastated by the contrast between her two sojourns in hospital, to be born and to die. It occurred to me that Gina might have reminded Daniel of Sarah, so I asked him and he agreed.

'I thought perhaps she did,' I commented. 'She reminds me of Sarah too.'

Daniel: 'Why did she remind you of Sarah?'

'Well she has the same friendly lively expression . . . Perhaps that's why you hit Sylvia, because you were cross that she isn't Sarah.'

'Yes . . . Did Sarah hit me?'

'I suppose she did sometimes, I don't remember. Children always fight. I know you and Sarah used occasionally to bite each other quite hard when you got cross with each other.'

This is the first time I have found a natural way of introducing some negative recollection of Sarah, the first time such a recollection has even occurred to me when I was talking to Daniel. (And of course hitting and biting are not exactly negative to him; they are enjoyable rebellion.) We had a long reminiscent talk, Daniel repeatedly prompting me – What else did Sarah do? What else that was good? What else did Sarah and me do that was naughty? He embroidered several of my stories with remembered details.

Daniel, 'Once when Kim [*the cat*] got into the fireplace,

did Sarah say, "Come out of that, Kim, you shouldn't be there"?'

'I don't know darling, I don't remember. Did she?'

'Yes.'

'Was I there?'

'No, no one was there except Sarah and me.'

When I went to tell Erwin dinner was ready, Daniel went with me and waited till Erwin came to the kitchen. He asked to be 'frogged' – Sarah's game. Erwin thought that this showed I had been right in thinking Gina must have reminded him of Sarah.

This morning he got into bed with me for a while. He said that the ventilator looked like a fish bone. Then, 'Why weren't there any bones in the fish we had at Lorne?'

'The cook took them out to make the fish easier to eat.'

Daniel: 'We had fish and chips with Sarah when it was dark.'

We had indeed done this more than once. Erwin hated hotel meals, and when we were away, fish and chips, often eaten in the dark, was an alternative.

'Yes we did, and afterwards we went back to the hotel and I gave you and Sarah a bath before you went to bed.' This had been in April 1964.

Daniel: 'No, I don't mean that time. I mean the time we saw the grey tractor.' True, we had – on a previous occasion, in January 1964.

Daniel: 'Was it dark the time we saw the tractor?'

'It was nearly dark at the beginning and it got quite dark before we finished.'

Daniel has been very nice to Sylvia this morning, getting his bag of plastic ducks and fish to show her, and making her laugh.

September 9

One of the stories I told Daniel two nights ago, at his request, was about him and Sarah playing chasey on their bikes. Last night Sylvia was fretful and I walked her round the path in her pram. Daniel got on his tricycle and started to chase after us, pedalling furiously. I joined in the game, calling out, 'Look out, he's going to catch us up. Here he comes, going like mad.' He had a smile of happiness. He said several times, 'You say to Sylvia, "Look at your big brother on his bike."' It seemed a valiant effort to recapture the gaiety of those games with Sarah, just as occasionally he has tried to play chasey indoors and to involve me in it. The games don't last long and are not repeated often because it just isn't and can't be the same, in spite of Daniel's surges of cheerfulness.

September 10

Last December Daniel christened each of the three kittens Messo Messo. Since then, 'messo' has become the family word for cat. A few days ago when we were passing an Esso station Daniel said, 'Look, there are two tigers' heads, so it's a Messo station.'

His great generosity when playing his favourite games: 'I'm making a cake for you.' 'What sort of fish would you like? A barracuda? Here's a barracuda.' This has been a favourite game for months.

I bought him a bird book from town yesterday. He disappeared with it for an hour into Mama's room, and spent time looking at it with her again this morning. He loves to know the names of creatures.

He stood on Mama's bed, looking very pleased with himself, and announced, 'I'm a bronze grackle.' Then, to Margaret, 'I'm a grackle and you're a cassowary.'

A few days ago he asked repeatedly, 'Where's the book with the maribou stork?'

September 17
A story told by Mrs Taverner, the nursery school teacher. She was talking to the children about firemen and asked if anyone knew why they wore those wide leather belts.

'I asked Feddy, and he replied, "I'm more of an expert on animals."'

September 20
Until this morning Daniel had not seen a power tool, although he had heard about them. He included a power tool in the list of tools he was proposing to give Erwin the other day.

'When I give you a power tool, you'll be able to go zzzz and there's a hole.'

This morning he saw Erwin using a power tool he has borrowed, and was delighted. He came upstairs to tell me about it when I was in the shower. I have gently discouraged him from coming in when I'm in the shower, by saying that I like to be by myself, and also that if he opens the bathroom door it makes a draught. This morning he asked me to open the door, which I did. I put my head round the shower curtain while he told me about the power tool, very pleased.

Then he said, 'I'm going now. I'll shut the door,' and did, all very discreetly.

Grandpa reported that Daniel had given him a long description at breakfast about spiders, and at the end he said, 'I've just about had spiders!' He said the same thing to me yesterday, following it up with 'What have you just about had, Mummy?'

September 25
While I was lifting Daniel to show him something I got cramp in the abdomen, as I often do since the operation. I gasped a little and put him down, then said reassuringly, 'It's only a bit of cramp in my tum.'
   Daniel: 'Does cramp make you die?'

At the end of September we had a holiday. We went to Sydney, where Erwin had a sculpture exhibition, and after the opening drove up the coast of New South Wales as far as Coff's Harbour, in the banana-growing belt near the Queensland border. There were good moments, but for me the general atmosphere was sombre. I still thought constantly about Sarah, and Sylvia was a preoccupying and not particularly gay presence. Daniel didn't often make-believe Sarah was with us, as he had the previous year, but much of the time he wasn't particularly ebullient either. Nevertheless there were big new experiences for him – his first flight since he was a baby (Erwin had driven to Sydney and I flew up with the children); and the Manly aquarium, with a vast cylindrical tank in the sea in which shoals of fish swam round in more-or-less natural conditions; they included a huge groper and a number of sharks. We went there several times; Daniel studied the fish seriously through the viewing portholes and was quickly able to identify many more than we could.

Aunt Nell died while were away; Betty decided not to attempt to let me know, so we got back only after the funeral. I must have told Daniel about her death at some stage, but I don't remember doing so.

October 25
Daniel seldom now asks why Sarah died, or where she is, but he refers to her often – to places where they were together, and to her possessions – 'Sarah's snake book'. The book is in pieces, and he asked me to buy him another one 'at the same shop where you bought Sarah's'. Other requests:

'One day can we go to the beach where Sarah and I looked for starfish in the rockpools?'

'One day can we go and cook a fish on the beach at the same beach where we cooked a fish when Sarah was alive?'

A memory of a different kind. During our recent holiday we drove to a surf beach. It was a sunny day, and as we turned a bend, the whole wide glittering expanse of ocean appeared in front of us from the cliff top. From the back seat Daniel called out Sarah's chant, 'Marvellous, marvellous, marvellous!', copying exactly the intonation of her teasing take-off of our exclamations of wonder. He has never done this except in appropriate circumstances.

Erwin reported that Daniel said to him, 'I can't remember Christmas when Sarah was here.'

November 8

Lately Daniel has been very concerned with health and death, asking such questions as, 'What can you do that would make you vomit or die? Would you vomit or die if you ate too much ice-cream?' Today I gave him a Golden Library book about the human body, because he has been asking me what various organs look like.

Daniel: 'Is there a picture that shows you what someone looks like when they're dead?'

'No, but you know what a dead person looks like because you saw Sarah when she was dead.'

'But I don't remember what she looked like.'

November 11

Daniel has had a very cheerful weekend, playing happily and boisterously in the garden, talking at great length to Mama (fantasies about fishing), showing off briefly but gleefully to Sylvia, and in the evenings teasing and defying Erwin and me. He has been more consistently cheerful than I can remember since Sarah died.

He is ambivalent towards Sylvia – 'I don't want her to choke' (she has had a bad cough), and 'Say to her look at your big brother catching a fish.' But to me: 'Why didn't you leave Sylvia in Sydney?' and to Erwin: 'Why did you let Mummy get a baby?'

He hasn't talked of Sarah often. Yesterday I showed Erwin a dress I had bought for Sylvia. Daniel said he wanted to wear a dress, and although I said boys don't wear dresses, he ran upstairs to get one of Sarah's and asked me to put it on. I took off his pyjamas and put the dress on – Sarah's brilliant orange cotton embroidered with white medallions. He looked very happy and climbed roughly and cheerfully on to Erwin. When I took the dress off, he ran and got another, and I put that on him too. But he made no mention of the fact that they were Sarah's dresses.

He turns to Erwin more often than to me for company and fantasy. He accepts that I like to sleep a bit later in the morning than he does, but he seeks out Erwin even when I ask him not to, as I did yesterday. It is usually I who sit with him while he goes to sleep, but last night he said he didn't want me, he wanted Daddy; in the end he was so tired that he fell asleep without either of us. But if I disappear and he doesn't know where I have gone, or even sometimes if I have simply gone to another part of the house after telling him where I am going, he gets too upset to look for me and starts to cry.

During October and November I made only these few notes, which are of a more general character than usual, and then none until the end of the year. Something else was claiming my attention – I had become aware of a serious crisis in my sister Betty's life which had plunged her into bewilderment and despair. I spent many hours talking to her, and was continuously worried and concerned about her. I noted, in another diary, that for the first time since Sarah's death, something else seemed more vivid and important than my inner engagement with my dead daughter.

Betty died early in December of an overdose of sleeping tablets. Her death left me feeling numb and exhausted. It was soon after this that I began to think more persistently about abandoning the plan to adopt Sylvia, although I didn't come to an immediate decision.

For Daniel Betty's death must have been a new and terrible blow. She lived nearby, he used to see her often, and she had an easy, affectionate, confidential, cheerful way with him. After those who lived in the house, she was the person closest to him. But I have no memory of how I told him of her death, nor of his immediate reaction.

December 30
Daniel: 'What do you do if your baby dies?'

'I don't understand darling. What do you mean?'

'I mean what do you do if your baby dies?'

'Do you mean what do you do with its body?'

'Yes.' It is the first time I have felt that Daniel was asking this question, although I have been expecting it for a long while.

'Well when somebody dies they've left their body and they never come back to it again.' (Several days ago he had asked 'Why when you die don't you come alive again?') 'All that's left is their body. It's not them. It can't see or feel or move. So you either bury it or you burn it.

When we went to see Sarah's body in hospital, Sarah wasn't there any more; it was only her body. We had Sarah's body burned.'

Daniel: 'Could Sarah feel it?'

'No, she couldn't feel it.'

'Why didn't you let me touch Sarah's body in hospital?' (I hadn't prevented or forbidden his touching her, I simply hadn't thought of suggesting it.)

I started to describe Sarah's funeral, wanting to explain that although the body was no longer the person, we still kept some of the same feelings towards it and wanted to treat it as if it were someone we loved. But Dan had had enough, and interrupted my account with a question about the wheels of a model airplane. He loses interest immediately whenever I try to speak about love or memory.

Later the same day, Daniel: 'Is the baby-home where Sylvia came from for giving babies to people who haven't got any of their own?'

'No, it's really for giving a home to babies who haven't got a home of their own.'

'Why haven't they?'

'Oh, there are a lot of reasons. Their mummy and daddy might be dead, or they might be sick and not able to look after the baby, or they mightn't have enough money to look after it, or the mummy might have to work and not be able to look after it. Sometimes after a while the mummy and daddy get a home of their own and then they take their baby back from the baby-home. And sometimes if they can't get a home for the baby, it is given to people who haven't got any children of their own.'

Daniel: 'Are Sylvia's mummy and daddy dead?'

'No.'

'What are their names?'

'I don't know their names, I only know the name of the woman who runs the baby-home.'

'Why didn't Sylvia's mummy and daddy keep her?'

I started to explain that they weren't married, and couldn't get married because her daddy was married to someone else. But Dan broke off and started to play with his airplanes.

1966

January 12

Daniel: 'Where are Aunty Betty and Sarah now?'

I started to answer that I didn't know, that their spirits had left their bodies and some people thought, etc. But he interrupted, showing that he didn't want that sort of answer.

'Are they in their coffins?'

'No, not now. They were put in coffins, that is their bodies were put in coffins, but after that they were burned, the body and the coffin. But it wasn't Aunty Betty or Sarah, only their bodies, because they had died.'

'Can you feel the fire when you are burned?'

'No, you can't feel anything when you are dead.'

'Can you feel the earth on your eyes when they bury you?'

'No. When you're dead you don't feel anything at all.'

January 13

Daniel to Erwin, in the kitchen: 'Why do you kill flies when they like to live?'

January 19

I talked to Daniel about Betty's death, and about Aunty Nell's. He asked a string of dead-pan questions: Was Aunty Betty burned? Was Sarah burned? Was Aunty Nell burned? When I replied that Aunty Nell had been buried, why was she buried? Why was Sarah burned and not buried?

'When they burned Aunty Betty, why did they burn the coffin too? That's just a waste. Why didn't they just take the body and shove it into the fire?'

I don't attempt much in the way of answers to such questions – say I don't know, or that it's a custom. On the burning of the coffin, I tried to explain that it was connected with people's grief, and with hiding that it was a person's body that was being burned. I didn't feel that this was successful, and Daniel didn't listen. As always when I talk about feelings, he stopped paying attention, and played with his blocks.

January 23

Much of the time Fed pays very little attention to Sylvia. He rarely makes any mention of her when she isn't present. When she is, there is fairly marked ambivalence. On the one hand, frequent minor physical assaults – sudden pinches, slaps and hair-pulls, especially if I am there but have momentarily looked away. But he often smiles very joyfully while watching her. The role he relishes most is that of big brother and future big brother.

He says to me things like, 'Say to Sylvia, "Your big brother can swim, Sylvia. You can't swim, but when you get older your big brother will teach you."'

Or, 'Say to Sylvia, "Your big brother is climbing a tree."'

He always wants me to be the one to tell Sylvia, insisting on it even when I point out that she can hear him just as well as she can me.

Several times he has asked, 'Why doesn't Sylvia look like Sarah?'

Since Betty's death, I had again been debating the question of Sylvia's future. I hadn't made much progress in learning to love her, and the weight of exhaustion that descended on me then made the task of looking after her for years to come seem an insupportable burden. I conjured up again that vision of the two children as gleeful allies against the grown-up world, but now it failed to outbalance my weariness, and the tepidity of my affection for poor Sylvia.

I went to see Sister Considine, anticipating a hard fight to justify handing Sylvia back like a parcel, but she agreed immediately. Before the determined date, Sister Considine reported that she had found a family who would make Sylvia welcome and happy. I won't give her persuasive reasons, in case they lead to Sylvia's identification. She is of course no longer Sylvia, just as she had left behind an earlier name when she came to us. Sister Considine had told me enough about her own deviousness in answering the enquiries of natural mothers to make me sceptical, but perhaps her story was true. She had a deep faith in the benevolence of Providence, and remarked that my year of fostering had been lucky, because a year earlier this new home had not been available.

February 2

Last Thursday I told Daniel, without premeditation, that we were planning to return Sylvia to the baby-home.

Daniel: 'Why?'

'After Sarah died we all felt very lonely and sad, and I thought it would be happier for all of us, for you and me and Daddy, if we had another baby. I thought we would all get to love her. But I don't love this baby like I do you and Sarah, and I don't think I could ever feel she really belonged to us. So I think it would be better for her if the baby-home finds another family who can really love her and think of her as their very own.'

Something like this. It sounds lame, and it sounded lame to me at the time. Fed wasn't impressed, and broke

in before I had finished with a question about snakes or
ships.

Neither of us mentioned the subject for three days.
Then on Sunday,

Daniel: 'Why did you say that you were going to take
Sylvia back to the baby-home?'

'Because that's what I'm going to do.'

'But I like making her laugh.'

'You'll have time to make her laugh because I'm not
going to take her back just yet.'

'But I want to make her laugh for always, and I want to
teach her things when she gets bigger.'

February 8

Daniel: 'If you look at the sun for a long while, do you go
blind?'

'No.'

'But Iris [*the nurse*] said you do.'

'Well Iris may believe it, but it's not true, it's an old
wives' tale.' I had tried to explain a few days before what
an old wives' tale was, when Mama told him that if you
had hiccups they stopped if you got a fright.

Daniel: 'Don't you ever tell me an old wives' tale.
Because I don't want you ever to tell me anything that
isn't true.'

'I never will tell you anything that I know isn't true. I
might make a mistake, or believe something is true when it
isn't, but I won't tell you that something is true when I
know it's not.'

That was yesterday. Fed reverted to it this morning,
asking me never to tell him anything that wasn't true,
'because then I might believe something that isn't true.' I
think this may be connected with the fate of Sylvia. It is
nearly a week since I told him we were going to return her.

He has asked me twice since, whether we are going to return her, and I have said yes but given no details about when; nor has he asked. But he may feel uncertain about what is going to happen, and afraid of being misled.

Just before we took Sylvia back, we visited a couple we had only recently met. The wife admired Sylvia as she lay in her carrycot on the floor, and commented that we must feel very thankful to have her. 'Not really,' I replied flatly. 'In fact I don't think I can go through with the adoption. I'm going to give her back.' 'Well in that case,' our new friend replied immediately, 'I would like you to meet our son. We adopted him twenty-seven years ago and it has never worked. He still seems like a stranger.'

February 14
I left Sylvia with Sister Considine three days ago, after telling Daniel the day before. Several times since, he has said things like, 'Mummy, don't you ever ever ever tell me something that isn't true.'

On Saturday, I said to him, 'I wonder what Sylvia is doing now. Are you sad that I took her back to the baby-home?'

Daniel: 'Yes. Why when you die can you never come back to life again?'

He has not made any protest about Sylvia. During the weekend he has been in very cheerful and boisterous spirits, and still is now, Monday. He has made only two references to her. On Saturday he said, 'I can hear the baby crying.' On Sunday Gina was here and I overheard him telling her, 'Our baby has gone back to the baby-home.'

February 16

Daniel: 'I want Sylvia to come back. I want her to stay here until she is old enough to play with me.'

'She wouldn't be old enough for quite a long while.'

'How long would it be until she is old enough to go to the school I go to?'

'Quite a long while, two years.'

Daniel: 'How long is two years?'

But when I attempted an explanation he lost interest and left the kitchen.

March 13

We made an excursion to Rye back beach yesterday with June and Helen Philipp. Dan laughed with a vigorous gaiety that reminded me of him and Sarah together. On the way home, the two children lay down in the back of the car with a rug over them, as Dan and Sarah used to. The outing must have reminded him too of the days when Sarah was alive, because after we dropped June and Helen, he knelt up and chanted 'Faster, faster!' from the back seat. This morning he raced cheerfully and defiantly round the house in the old circle from the chasey games – two acted-out recollections of the days with Sarah that he has not done for a long time.

A few days ago he said to me, 'Mummy, don't you ask Daddy to give you a seed because I don't want another baby.'

March 27

Daniel, with a happy grin: 'When Sarah died, why didn't we use her for bait?'

'I don't know. There are plenty of other things for bait.'
'But I mean when she was quite dead?'
'Dad and Mum wouldn't have liked it.'
Looking genuinely puzzled: 'Why not?'
'I don't know. She wouldn't have known about it, but we wouldn't have liked it.'

May 4
Daniel has a cold and is staying home from school. He asked to wear one of Sarah's dresses, which I put on over his own clothes because I didn't want to undress him. I can see him from my balcony, a lonely figure crossing the lawn and climbing the plum tree, both Sarah and Daniel, with her plaid 'school dress' over his own blue corduroy trousers.

May 22
Daniel still talks a lot about Sarah. Questions about her last day and her death – When she was given the penicillin injection was she already in hospital? What sort of ice-cream did she eat on that day? And joyful questions about outings: Did the two of them take buckets to collect starfish at Apollo Bay? Did they first fill their buckets with water? Did I walk down to the rock pools with them?

Two memories which he has produced recently:
While I was dressing a cut finger for him: 'Once Sarah had to have two pieces of sticking plaster, one on each knee. She showed them to me when we were having our bath.'
To Erwin in the kitchen, as he unscrewed the top of the pepper grinder: 'Did Sarah do this?'
Erwin: 'Yes, she did. That's how the washer got lost.'

This was the last note about Daniel that I made while we were still in Australia. They had become infrequent since Betty died, since I abandoned the hope that Sylvia might become part of our family, and since Daniel's knowledge of Sarah's death had been completed by learning that her body was burned. In September 1966 we started on our return journey to England, slowly, with an air ticket that allowed us to make long stops in Hong Kong, Cambodia, Greece and Vienna. Daniel left the places that were saturated with memories of Sarah, and entered a period of intense new experience.

During our three-week stay in Hong Kong he had an extra-ordinary outburst of creativity, filling sketch-book after sketch-book with vigorous and varied drawings of the ships that filled Hong Kong harbour. Some of them were crewed by a family of three cats. As we returned to the hotel one afternoon after a ferry trip to an outlying island, 'I want to draw', said Feddo, not stopping to take off his coat.

'He's doomed to be an artist!' Erwin commented. 'That impatience to express what he has seen through drawing!'

Throughout the journey, I continued to live the double life of the mourner, relishing the new sights but simultaneously continuing all the time to think about her, to wonder how it was possible that we could be making such a journey without her, to scribble notes about rediscovering obvious truths for the umpteenth time. But the notes contain no record that Daniel talked about Sarah or recalled her life in any way.

While we had remained in Australia, outings and sojourns away from home had always evoked memories of her, but this journey was vastly different, from its initial day-long flight over deserts and oceans to its proliferation of exotic scenes. Many of these answered to his own particular passions: tanks of tropical fish in the Hong Kong markets, water buffalo in the Cambodian paddy fields, a mountain forest alive with brilliant butterflies and monkeys swinging from tree to tree by their long black arms. By the Mekong River a friendly teenage boy draped live snakes around his neck. On a wharf in Crete he helped to land a huge catch of shining garfish.

Two years before, during our first trip to Sydney without her, I had thought, 'She is being buried under new experience,' and had felt a piercing stab of despair. For me, the reflection was premature, for I was to live in her constant presence for many more years. For Daniel however it was true this time, a transformation to be accepted with gratitude, which must have been given strong impetus by the crowding impressions of Hong Kong, Cambodia and Bangkok, of Greece, Crete and wintry Vienna, and by our eventual arrival at a house that for him held no memories of Sarah.

Over the next few years I added an occasional page, unsystematically, to the Daniel and Sarah file, but most of them are only about Daniel. There are just three entries in which Sarah is named.

1967

March 23

Daniel was very disappointed at missing a television programme last night, when I forgot to remind him until it was too late. He has come into my room several times in tears.

Finally I said with some exasperation, 'But I can't make it yesterday, that's one thing I can't possibly ever do, bring back yesterday.'

Of course I thought of Sarah, who was already present in my mind because I have been giving him reading lessons from the books I bought for her. Did something in my voice recall her to Daniel too?

Almost the next thing he said was, 'Was Sarah older than I am now when she died?'

July 22

Feddo has a terror of dirt, germs and poison which perhaps is common at his age, but which I think is probably also linked with his experience of Sarah's death. He knows, as not many children do, what it is for someone he loved to disappear, suddenly and forever, in a way that can't really be explained. Who can say when such a thing might not happen to him?

For example I caught a jellyfish for him at the beach in a plastic cup. He refused for days to drink from the cup, even after I had washed it thoroughly before his eyes, in case the jellyfish had left traces of poison in it. Later he was playing wildly with the foxgloves we had picked in Somerset, flailing them around and knocking all the flowers off. He wouldn't stop when I asked him to, and finally I said, 'You shouldn't do that. Foxgloves have poison in them.' He put them down immediately and insisted on having his face and hands washed. Then he noticed that some water had spilled on his pyjama top and insisted that I change it.

But she still lives for him, as for none of our friends. During the holiday he asked me who was my favourite cat. I said Feddo and Daddy both were. He asked immediately, 'And Sarah?'

[*Sarah's name for Daniel has survived in the more robust Australian form of Feddo – as in commo, reffo, and wino.*]

August 7

I was talking to Enid about where her grandchildren had been born, and Feddo asked where he had been born. I said, 'In a little hospital in London. I'll show you one day.' Feddo: 'And where was Sarah born?' In that company it sounded shockingly outspoken.

1970

The last note in the file was made more than two years later, more than five after Sarah's death. It brings the Diary to a fortuitously neat and ambiguous end.

January 15
I have been reading Daniel at bedtime *The Mouse and his Child*, which has a lot of talk about territory and the mouse-child's desire for his own.

Daniel said, 'We haven't got a territory.'

'Yes we have, we've got this flat.'

'No. But,' whispering, 'when we buy the house we'll have a territory of our own.' We are negotiating to buy the house in which we live, and have told him, but asked him not to say anything to anyone else.

He went on, 'Who will I leave it to when I die?'

'You'll probably have children of your own then. You'll leave it to them. And to your wife.'

'Perhaps,' Daniel concluded cheerfully, 'my wife will die before I do.'

AFTERWORD

It was many years after that before we talked again about Sarah's death, and then it was as equals, speculating on the difference having an older sister might have made to him. And it is as an equal, prepared to accept his share of sacrifice, that he has agreed to this privacy-invading publication, for which I thank him.

Rereading the Diary yet again, after the work of preparing it for publication has given it greater distance, it struck me that in these conversations about Sarah's death I was over-controlled, treating it too calmly as an event in the natural order. If I had at least once given way to tear-stricken grief and we had wept together, it might have given Daniel a truer impression of what I felt, and shown him that for all of us Sarah's death was a terrible catastrophe quite outside the normal course of life. But one can only behave in the way that is natural to oneself, and perhaps it would simply have been frightening. On the other hand, staunch unbeliever as I remain, I have quite abandoned my misgivings about the angels story, which seems to me now absolutely appropriate as a temporary mythologizing of a truth most adults do not wish to face.

However much one might talk, or even write books, the inner image of the beloved dead becomes with time less and less shareable. This must be even more true when the death occurred during the forgotten first years. The conversations recorded here, though, must have helped to ensure that Sarah's death lives on in Daniel with the heaviness of human sorrow rather than with the explosive terror of nightmare. Certainly his attitude towards his own death seems to be one of cool detached acceptance combined with prudence – so long as that doesn't get in the way of what he wants to do. But it is not only her death that inevitably remains with him.

Some time before Sarah died, we visited a wild stretch of ocean beach with Cecily. It was a sunny day in early spring, and against a backdrop of the mighty, restless sea the children raced and tumbled down the sand dunes with Cecily, whom they loved. Looking at their bright faces, Erwin remarked, 'What a pity they won't remember any of this!' 'But it won't be lost,' Cecily replied. 'It will always be a part of them – it's the most important way they *could* remember.' If the sadness of Sarah's death remains part of Daniel, so also does the happiness of the three years they shared.

Daniel and Sarah in the mountains behind the
small timber-milling township of Powelltown,
where we often went on Sundays and never
saw another soul. *Erwin Fabian*

A sisterly reprimand during a picnic
from the tailgate of our pink Holden
station-wagon . *Erwin Fabian*

Mother and children in
the Tambo river during our first
bush wandering. In the early photographs,
Sarah and Daniel nearly always remain close
to each other, although occupied with their
separate concerns. *Erwin Fabian*